SHIPWRECKS

AND OTHER MARITIME DISASTERS

of the

MAINE COAST

SHIPWRECKS

AND OTHER MARITIME DISASTERS

of the

MAINE COAST

TARYN PLUMB

Down East Books

Camden, Maine and Guilford, Connecticut

Down East Books

An imprint of The Rowman & Littlefield Publishing Group, Inc.
4501 Forbes Blvd., Ste. 200
Lanham, MD 20706
www.rowman.com

Distributed by NATIONAL BOOK NETWORK

British Library Cataloguing in Publication Information available

Library of Congress Cataloging-in-Publication Data available

ISBN 978-1-60893-724-0 (paper : alk. paper)
ISBN 978-1-60893-725-7 (electronic)

∞™ The paper used in this publication meets the minimum requirements of American National Standard for Information Sciences—Permanence of Paper for Printed Library Materials, ANSI/NISO Z39.48-1992.

To all those souls who have been lost to the sea—may you have found peace.
And to all the sirens and muses alike, who crave oblivion.

CONTENTS

INTRODUCTION

"Si recte calculum ponas, ubique naufragium est."
"If you reckon correctly, shipwreck is everywhere."
—Gaius Petronius Arbiter

"There's always a siren, singing you to a shipwreck."
—Caitlin R. Kiernan

Just imagine what it's like.

The fracas and tumult of the sea; the insistent wind stinging and biting; the water rising, consuming, relentless; the intertwining panic, helplessness, and hopelessness. Then, finally, the dreadful resigning to fate.

Shipwrecks are lonely, solemn places—one of the greatest tragedies suffered (and, ultimately, created) by humankind.

And, being as old as seafaring itself, they provide an unrivaled, enduring human drama.

For centuries, we have been captivated by the catastrophic, mysterious nature of shipwrecks—which remain forever entwined with the ocean's vast, spurning, unforgiving nature.

Morbidly romanced by the idea of being "lost at sea," humankind across its existence has immortalized shipwrecks in literature, including our oldest and greatest works—*The Odyssey* by Homer, for example, William Shakespeare's "Twelfth Night," Herman Melville's *Moby Dick*, and Daniel Defoe's *Robinson Crusoe*. Artists from the Renaissance to modern day have chronicled their catastrophic demise in paintings, while bards captured their loss in forlorn song.

During the late nineteenth and early twentieth centuries, it was common for New England excursionists to travel from all over to view stranded, wrecked ships whose ruin had made spectacular headlines.

Consider the public's enduring fascination with the RMS *Titanic* (whose designation as "unsinkable" was not only jinxing, but indicative of man's misled hubris when it comes to seafaring). Her sinking in 1912 during her maiden voyage—and the discovery of her halved hulk seventy-three years later, in 1985, more than 12,000 feet below the North Atlantic Ocean—has spawned dozens of books, television shows, and movies, the most notable of which remains one of the highest-grossing films of all time.

Maine, for its part, has proved an integral set piece for many a shipwreck drama: Given the scabrous nature of the state's coastline, combined with the unruly Atlantic, and the area's rich history of ship-building, coastwise commerce and trade, the waters off the Maine coast are a literal graveyard of ships.

Untold Tragedy

Hundreds of thousands of shipwrecks, both big and small, have occurred across the long span of maritime history. The oldest-dated intact wreck dates to 400 BCE. Remarkably, the 2,400-year-old downed ship was discovered in 2018, more than 6,500 feet below the Black Sea. The wreck has been well-preserved, due to the anoxic (oxygen-free) nature of the eastern European sea. As seafaring was instrumental to the development of civilization, and the practice of sailing dates to several thousand years BCE, we can wisely assume that the first tragedy took place right around that time, or not long thereafter. Still, we will never know for sure when the first-ever ship-wreck occurred. Over the thousands of years that man has attempted to govern the seven seas, the wrecks that have been reported represent but a fraction of the number of vessels that were actually downed. The true number remains as baffling as the ocean herself.

Maine serves as a microcosm of all this; as local maritime historian Edward Rowe Snow described it, "so crowded are the archives of New England history with tales of not hundreds, but thousands, of ship-wrecks." The well-respected researcher also pointed out that, between 1790 and 1850, three out of every five sailors in New England were drowned at sea.

As his fellow historian, William P. Quinn, aptly assented of the hazy history: "The first maritime accident in New England was probably never entered into the record books. It could have been one of the early Norse explorers stranded on the shoals near Nantucket, or driven by a storm onto the rocky coasts of Maine or Rhode Island."

But there is, at least, a baseline: More than 1,600 shipwrecks have been documented in Maine waters since Europeans first anchored along her shores. Most of these occurred within five miles of the coast, according to Warren Riess, a maritime historian and archaeologist, and were concentrated near ports in shallow water beset by impediments such as rocks and sandbars.

Still, Riess notes, the actual total is likely closer to 2,500 or 3,000 wrecks (again, though, that remains pure assumption). Many wrecks were never reported because they were small sailing vessels owned by local fishermen. Others merely sailed off and disappeared, with no survivors to tell the tale of what happened to them. Moreover, reporting was not a habit, nor a required practice. In fact, owners or representatives of wrecked U.S. vessels were not required to provide detailed reports until Congress deemed it so in 1874. Following the decree, any vessel involving a loss of life, or damage that would impact its seaworthiness, was required to provide records to their appropriate collector of customs—either where the vessel was registered or where the accident had occurred.

Meanwhile, the chronicling of sea disasters was often impeded by conflicting stories, unreliable witnesses, and sailors prone to exaggeration—not to mention their curious manner of speaking. As Quinn drolly asserted, "the sailors vernacular bodes ill for factual information."

Take a sailor's description of an early twentieth-century wreck southwest of Nantucket Island, for instance: "We was going along all fluking when the wind drawed ahead," he told *The New York Times*. "We trimmed sail, and in fore and mizzen tor'garns'l, when a bit of sea making' of her yaw. 'Mind yer luff, you soger,' sings out the old man,' an' as he says this, one of the jib guys parted and swung the boom, for ours were swinging booms and had the for'd guy and the after guy fitted in ne, with a cuckold's neck around the boom end."

"Are yer followin' on me sir?"

Speaking of sailors and their unique manners and methods, many wrecks in Maine waters were later chocked up to long-held superstitions: the name of the boat had been changed; sharks had been sighted nearby; women were aboard; whistling had broken out; the vessel had set out on a Friday (a sacred day for Christians, the day Jesus Christ had been crucified) or on a Thursday (the day of Thor, the god of thunder and storms); or, the morning sky had flamed red.

In any case, Maine's 3,500 miles of flinty, treacherous coastal terrain—with its dozens of inlets, coves, and craggy fingers of land clawing at the sea—have spelled disaster for countless ships. Even the islands just off Maine's shores seem to foreshadow the dangers of the sea with ominous names like Deadman Ledge, Folly Ledge, Devil's Island, Hell Gate (there's an upper and a lower one of these), Brimstone Island, Burial Island, and Bailey's Mistake.

Over the centuries, ships of all sizes and types have capsized upon striking concealed ledges and rocks amidst storms; gone down in heavy seas and cloaking fog; inexplicably collided with one another, rocks, or even large whales; borne the brunt of accidental fire or explosion; been plagued by boiler or structural failure; lost sails and rudders; or experienced a breakdown of essential propulsion equipment. During war times, ships were struck by torpedoes or mines; were lured ashore by treachery; or were deliberately sunk or "scuttled" by their own crews to prevent enemy capture.

Human error and circumstance was another major factor that shouldn't be discounted: Ships were at the mercy of their crewmembers as they dealt with illness, injury, exhaustion, drunkenness, incompetence, and inexperience. Then there were the occasional instances of infighting, sabotage, and mutiny. Early on, all of these circumstances were exacerbated by the fact that no buoys or lighthouses were present to provide valuable guides or points of reference.

Try as we might to categorize these maritime disasters into simple boxes, each and every wreck—as we will explore in ensuing chapters—was unique in its destruction and demise.

History to the Rescue

As is the case across the course of history, seafaring was born of equal parts trial and error.

As soon as humans launched the first crudely-built dory into the unknown waters of the sea, shipwrecks became a common occurrence. Once it became clear that such disasters were not going to cease—no matter how skilled the sailor or sophisticated the equipment—lifesaving efforts quickly commenced.

The earliest guiding lights and sentinels leading sailors to safety were said to be controlled fires set along rocky coastlines, or lanterns hung from moored boats. But it didn't take mariners long to realize that the higher up the light was set, the farther it could be seen, so the practice evolved to setting bonfires ablaze atop taller and taller precipices.

Following the example set by their European ancestors—who, in turn, were inspired by the ancient Egyptians and Greeks—the first lighthouse in the American colonies was erected in 1716 on Little Brewster Island in Boston Harbor. Boston Light's 89-foot tower still stands today, keeping guard at one of the country's oldest continually active ports.

By 1771, eleven colonial lighthouses had been put into service, spanning the coastline from Portsmouth, New Hampshire to Savannah, Georgia. Meanwhile, amidst Maine's burgeoning maritime and shipping trade—which not surprisingly led to shipwrecks on a daily basis—the state's first lighthouse was put into service in 1791. Portland Head Light was commissioned by President George Washington, who took a strong interest in establishing lighthouses up and down the east coast.

Dozens of lighthouses were built all along Maine's watery borders—spanning from York at the tip of New Hampshire to Lubec at the cusp of Canada. Sixty-five of them remain today, some still in operation, while others have been decommissioned and taken over by private parties and historical bodies.

Still, these structures weren't always able to prevent disaster. In 1786, the Massachusetts Humane Society was formed to provide relief for sailors cast ashore. The organization built small sheds furnished with canned foods, first aid kits, flares, and a fireplace complete with fuel along remote and desolate shorelines. The first of these "charity houses" was built in 1789 at Lovell's Island in Boston Harbor. But the Society didn't stop there: they also established, erected, and oversaw a network of eighteen lifeboat station facilities equipped with rescue gear along the coast of Massachusetts.

All these efforts would serve as the model for the United States Life-Saving Service, which was founded by the federal government in 1848. By 1838, the federal government had already established the Steam-Boat Inspection Service, which required that fire-fighting gear, lifeboats, and life jackets be kept aboard commercial seagoing vessels.

At first, the Life-Saving Service depended largely on the tireless work of volunteers. Then, in the early 1870s, Congress voted to appropriate $200,000 to reorganize the Service, purchase better equipment, build new stations, and employ experienced men to patrol shorelines and aid in rescue efforts.

As these "life savers" were known to proclaim: "The rule book says you've got to go out, it doesn't say anything about coming back!"

Over its sixty-seven year history, the Life-Saving Service's efforts saved more than 200,000 lives and $2 billion dollars' worth of property. Finally, in 1915, the Service merged with the longstanding U.S. Revenue Cutter Service—which had been established in 1790 to collect custom duties and taxes—to form the U.S. Coast Guard, which performs lifesaving duties to this day.

And, while the frequency of shipwrecks has greatly diminished with the advent of plane, train, and long-haul overland transport, not to mention improved shipbuilding methods, safety standards, and communication methods, it would be unwise to assume they would ever completely cease.

Perhaps, the following stories of tragedy and triumph, loss and salvation, can serve as cautionary tales and reminders of the sea's mighty dominance and will.

CURRENTS OF HISTORY

EARLY WRECKS AND THE GREAT COLONIAL HURRICANE

"Nothing ever begins. There is no first moment; no single word or place from which this or any other story springs."

—Clive Barker

Because history is so subjective (it is most often documented by the victorious and the successful) it is impossible to identify with any certainty the first major shipwreck along Maine's shores.

Undoubtedly, indigenous sailors and the first Viking explorers would have experienced the full brunt of the sea and Mother Nature working in vengeful tandem. But at present no evidence exists of specific wrecks—or they have yet to be unearthed.

One of the first ships said to be run aground in Maine belonged to none other than the world-renowned Samuel de Champlain. The founder of Quebec and the "Father of New France" inadvertently struck Mount Desert—one of Maine's northernmost, and largest, coastal islands—in 1604, but neither his ship nor his crew suffered any serious damage, so he continued on his enterprising way.

The first definitive, detailed account dates to 1624: that of *The Little James*, and dutifully recorded by William Bradford, governor of Plymouth Colony (modern-day Massachusetts). As he wrote, the Pilgrims went to "quite a little trouble" having a pinas (vessel) "new-masted and rigged" before sending it off for fishing purposes in the area of Damariscove in present-day Boothbay Harbor. However, while she was anchored along with many other ships newly-arrived from England, a strong storm hit, and she was driven against the island's jagged rocks. The violent action, Bradford wrote, "beat such a hole in her bulke, as a horse and cart might have gone in," then drove her into deep water, "wher she lay sunke." The captain, or master as Bradford referred to him, was drowned, "all her provision, salt, and what els was in her, was lost," but with great effort, the remainder of her human cargo survived.

As the vessel was sturdily-built, the Pilgrims placed numerous barrels around her at low tide, enabling them to float her to a cove where carpenters and cask-makers worked to make her seaworthy again. "She cost a great deale of money, in thus recovering her," Bradford noted; this included the purchase of new rigging and sails. He contributed his own funds and even though the ship returned to Plimoth, he lamented that he was never reconciled expenses "presented by the first Maine wreckers in history."

One of the most notorious "wreckers"—still, to this day—occurred just a little over a decade later. The Great Colonial Hurricane roared in off the Atlantic in August 1635, skirting the Virginia coast before passing directly over New England. Bradford, ever the prolific documenter, described it as "such a mighty storm of wind and rain as none living in these parts, either English or Indians, ever saw." Both he and John Winthrop, a leading figure in the Massachusetts Bay Colony, reported that the intense storm blew down thousands of trees—either uprooting them entirely or breaking them clear in half, as if standing twigs—and destroyed many houses and ripped ships free of their anchors. Further inland, tornadoes were also purportedly whipped into existence, wreaking their own destruction.

Modern-day meteorologists still categorize the hurricane as one of the most intense storms to ever make landfall in the recorded history of the region, though storms of similar magnitude would hit in 1723, 1815, and 1938.

Ultimately, this all proved treacherous for many settlers and mariners—and particularly disastrous for the ships *James* and *Angel Gabriel*. These vessels were two of a large fleet that carried Puritans from England to the New World during the "Great Migration" of the early-to-mid-1600s. Both ships had recently completed the long transatlantic voyage, having departed the mother country around the same time and from the same port in Bristol.

The 220-ton *James* held 100 passengers, including Richard Mather, his wife, four children, and father-in-law. Mather was traveling to the colonies to escape religious persecution and to begin a new life following his recent suspension from the Church of England; he had failed to conform to church expectations in conducting church services. In a strange turn of events, his son, Increase Mather, and grandson, Cotton Mather, would later become entwined with the history and mythos of the Salem Witch Trials. The *Angel Gabriel*, for its part, was larger, slower, and carrying an extra twenty tons of colonists and supplies. Despite this, the two vessels arrived at the New England coast around the same time. The *James* landed at the Isles of Shoals, an archipelago whose varying bumps and heaves of earth splay across the modern-day Maine and New Hampshire borders; the *Angel Gabriel* achored roughly seventy miles farther north, in the outer Pemaquid Harbor on Maine's midcoast.

After some slow going and failed attempts to seek shelter as the great storm blew in, the *James* eventually anchored along the Shoals—either Hog Island or Appledore Island, depending on the account. However, it proved but a brief safe haven: By daybreak, the ship was in a dire situation.

As the God-fearing Richard Mather described it, the Lord sent forth "a most terrible storm of rain and easterly wind, whereby we were in as much danger as, I think, ever people were."

Two of the ship's anchors were ripped free by the violent waves, while the third was cut by crewmen in "extremity and distress, to save the ship and their and our lives."

Anchors and cables quickly swallowed up by the sea, the last chance of survival was to unfurl their sails; but as Mather recounted, "the Lord let us see that our sails could not save us neither . . . for, by the force of the wind and rain, the sails were rent in sunder and split into pieces, as if they had been but rotten rags."

Now anchorless, sail-less, and but a wooden hulk prone to the whims of the storm, the ship was soon bearing down on "rocks of death." Mather, his family, and the other passengers and crew considered their time to be imminent, and began praying for their souls and salvation.

And, as Mather believed, it worked.

"In this extremity and appearance of death, as distress and distraction would suffer us, we cried unto the Lord, and he was pleased to have compassion and pity upon us; for by his overruling providence and his own immediate good hand, he guided the ship past the rock, assuaged the violence of the sea and wind and rain, and gave us a little respite to fit the ship with other sails, and sent us a fresh gale of wind."

The wind slackened and the ship escaped the rocky ledges of the Shoals. There was not one death or serious injury. This news of passing danger was related to Mather and other passengers hunkered in the gun room—upon hearing it, "how our hearts did then relent and melt within us!" Mather wrote. They quickly "burst into tears of joy amongst ourselves, in love onto our gracious God, and admiration of his kindness in granting to his poor servants such an extraordinary and miraculous deliverance."

Although battered—and its crew and passengers undoubtedly exhausted and weary—*James* made it to Boston Harbor a few days later.

"It was a day much to be remembered," Mather later espoused, "because on that day the Lord granted us a wonderful deliverance as, I think, ever people had, out of as apparent danger as I think ever people felt."

But *Angel Gabriel*, it seems, was not so divinely-touched.

The 240-ton galleon boasted quite the illustrious career: It was built in 1615 as *Starre*; then, two years later as *Jason*, it carried twenty-five cannons to Guiana as part of Sir Walter Raleigh's expedition to South America. Again, in 1619, it was purchased by English merchants and renamed *Angel Gabriel*. (This frequent name-changing was considered by some sailors to bring bad luck.) For several years it was a cargo-carrying vessel, and earned fame in 1627 when, off the coast of northern France, it repelled three attacking Spanish ships. This exploit spurred a ballad (and perhaps a jinx) of a "ship of brave command" whose "fight was so infamous, that all men's hearts doth fill. And make them cry, 'To sea, with the *Angel Gabriel*.'"

In its final—fatal—career, the ship became part of the Great Migration; its transatlantic voyage in 1635 was carrying would-be colonists to a 1,200-acre trading settlement in Pemaquid (on Maine's modern-day mid-coast). The *Gabriel*'s captain was believed to have been Robert Andrews, a native of Norwich, England, and the ship was said to have been loaded with sixteen guns as well as several tons of goods and personal belongings.

Upon reaching the settlement's harbor, many passengers disembarked to meet long-unseen family members and friends and to begin putting down their own roots. However, an unknown number remained aboard.

They were still aboard when, the following morning, the hurricane clamored in, bringing with it wild northeast winds that blew for hours, causing the tide in some places to rise twenty feet. The bellowing gale destroyed the prone ship, smashing it to bits and killing all on board. Most of its cargo and goods were also taken off by the sea.

Richard Mather, having survived his own ordeal, described the *Gabriel* as "burst to pieces and cast away in ye storme" while at anchor. Another writer, Thomas Vanburen Haines, ancestor to passenger Samuel Haines, wrote in 1902 that "during the storm the wind changed from north-east to north-west. The *Angel Gabriel*, probably now feeling the full force of the wind, was torn from her anchorage, and dashed to pieces upon the shore."

Later searches of archival records by historians revealed the names of just twenty-five of the ship's passengers. It remains unclear how many perished when it broke up and sunk that fateful morning.

In recent years, some divers have reported discovering lead bars on the sea floor near Pemaquid Harbor, but the exact "resting place" of the *Angel Gabriel* has never been found.

One survivor of the wreck was John Cogswell, a wealthy London merchant who sold his mills and real estate holdings before setting off for Pemaquid with his wife and several children. Another was a man identified as a Mr. Bailey; he had de-boarded the night before and was expecting to bring his wife to the "New World" once he had established himself. However, following the disaster he wrote a letter home describing the storm in detail. It was apparently so vivid that his wife was terrified to venture across the Atlantic to meet him; he, in turn, was too traumatized to make the journey home. And so, the years went by, as historian and maritime expert Edward Rowe Snow relates, "she in England, he in America, each hoping and praying that the other would make the journey across the water."

But neither did; they never saw one another again.

Theirs were two of the many hearts broken by the sea's unexpected fury.

2

AN ENCLAVE OF MISFORTUNE

BOON ISLAND

"Cannibals? Who is not a cannibal?"

—Herman Melville

They were gaunt, weak, sallow-eyed, barely suitable to be stick figures. Malnutrition and exposure had reduced their fingers and toes to claws; their prone skin and rotting fingernails could have peeled right off.

More than three weeks after being shipwrecked on an isle off the southern coast of Maine—without provisions, food, water, or adequate shelter—the castaways were, somehow, mercifully, alive. But not long after their rescue, they revealed the gruesome truth behind their means of survival: They had eaten the carpenter, soaking his flesh in saltwater, and supplementing the meat with bitter seaweed.

Cannibalism. By far, one of the most taboo of all human acts.

Sheer desperation and the need to survive led members of the *Nottingham Galley's* crew to eat one of their own when stranded on Boon Island in 1710.

Some would say the island's very location and landscape set the scene for horror and heartbreak. The tiny spot of land—spanning just 300 by 700 feet at low tide, and located six-and-a-half miles off Maine's southern coast—has been described as barren. It is perched barely ten feet above the high water mark, shrub-less, treeless, with soil not fertile enough for even the simplest of gardens.

"It nowhere shows the smallest part of natural soil," William C. Williams, longtime keeper at its equally desolate lighthouse, told author Robert Thayer Sterling. "It is hardly an island."

And the barely-isle has a grisly history consisting of numerous shipwrecks, drownings, mysterious deaths, ghosts, and other spectral entities.

One of the earliest legends involves the *Increase*, a trading vessel that dashed upon Boon's shores in 1682. The four surviving sailors toughed it out on the island for an entire month, living on what food they could find, mostly fish and pilfered gulls' eggs. Finally, they were rescued when natives rowed over from the mainland after spotting smoke from their bonfire.

Some credit those shipwrecked sailors for the island's name; upon rescue, they were said to have called it boon, for "lucky place." However, it was called either "Boone," or, more fittingly because of its ghastly history, "Bone" much earlier by settlers, including John Winthrop. The morbid case of the *Nottingham Galley* also spawned a tradition of fishermen leaving emergency rations on the island for any persons unlucky enough to be stranded in the future.

As a means to quell further disaster, the Boon Island lighthouse, originally built in 1812, was rebuilt in 1831, and again in 1855. Its numerous iterations are indicative of the ceaseless batterings it has endured from the sea and sky. Seen from a distance, the slim gray structure is striking in its height (the tallest light in Maine), appearing like a giant medieval tower: dark, ominous, unwelcoming, streaked black with years of brine.

Those who have spent time tending it have described its sheer desolation.

Young Annie Bell Hobbs, in the January 1876 issue of the children's magazine *Nursery*, described Boon Island as an outcropping of rock surrounded by the broad imposing Atlantic, "upon which I have been a prisoner, with the privilege of the yard, the past two years." The fourteen-year-old daughter of assistant keeper Edwin Hobbs, continued: "Now and then sails dot the wide expanse, reminding me that there is a world besides the little one I dwell in, all surrounded by water."

Williams, keeper for twenty-seven years beginning in 1885, also spoke of its isolation and the ocean's cruel devastation. Carrier pigeons were at times the only means of communication; soil had to be brought in from the mainland in buckets to create even the most meager of gardens (which were most often swept away by waves); and up in the sparse lantern room the only seat was an upturned box.

During violent storms the sea would completely overtake it, bashing down doors, flooding structures, and carrying away anything movable: giant boulders, hen coops, boardwalks. The tower swayed in brutal winds—which, as they howled through, created eerie sounds like "mad music from an Aeolian harp."

Williams also recalled bizarre instances in which disoriented birds and ducks flew into the tower during storms—sometimes so many that they could be picked up by the bushel.

"There were days when I first went to the station that I could not get away from the idea that I was the same as locked up in a cell," Williams said. "It was a funny experience to be on a place and know you couldn't get off if you wanted to."

The *Nottingham Galley*: A Fate Worse than Death

Which was precisely the case for the doomed crewmembers of the *Nottingham Galley*. Due to their acts, they survived to write several accounts describing their harrowing tale in stomach-churning detail.

The ill-fated ship was captained by John Deane, who before and after the ordeal was a polarizing figure—hailed by some, loathed by others. According to the 1870 writings of W.H.G. Kingston, Deane was born in 1679 in Nottingham, England. He started his working life as an apprentice butcher and drover, then purportedly poached local livestock before joining the Royal Navy at seventeen. It was said that was the first time he had ever set foot upon a boat. Nevertheless, he was promoted to captain by age twenty-five, following heroic acts at the Siege of Gibraltar in 1704, the twelfth during the War of the Spanish Succession. Five years later, he purchased his own ship, *Nottingham Galley*, named for his hometown. His brother Jasper and several other local men, including local businessman Charles Whitworth, assisted in the ship's funding and launching.

The 120-ton ship set out on its maiden voyage for the New England colonies on September 25, 1710, loaded with a cargo of cordage, butter, and cheese. The vessel was equipped with ten guns, and a crew of fourteen—including Deane's brother, Henry, and Whitworth's son, Miles. One legend also has it that on board were a packet of bloodred rubies—lost to the sea, never recovered, and a treasure-hunter's dream.

Almost immediately upon setting sail, Deane ran into a spate of bad weather. For more than eighty days, the sailors couldn't make out anything in any direction on the horizon. Historian and author Edward Rowe Snow described that "thick weather shut in." Like a veil, some might say.

Yet another two weeks passed—which must have seemed eternal torture for the men on board. Finally, the crew sighted land (the southern

Maine coast to the east of Piscataqua) in late November/early December. Being far north of their intended destination of Boston, the men attempted to sail the vessel south along the coast.

But a particularly ruthless blizzard descended, striking the ship with rain, hail, and snow, and leaving the men virtually blind for ten or twelve days, as Deane recalled later. Ceding to the weather, the men "handed," or ceased using, their sails, but the action came too late: The *Galley* abruptly cracked apart on the ragged ledges of Boon Island.

Deane and all of his crew survived despite the blackness and isolation, abandoning ship and struggling up the wet, icy ledges to dry land.

"I threw myself with all the strength I had toward the rock; but it being low water, and the rock extremely slippery, I could get no hold, and tore my fingers, hands, and arms in the most deplorable manner, every wash of the sea fetching me off again, so that it was with the utmost peril and difficulty that I got safe on shore at last," Deane wrote.

Many of the men "ran the same hazards," he noted. Some were said to have hastily assembled pieces of the foremast to create a crude plank to crawl across, thus escaping the frigid gauntlet.

Ultimately, they were "joyful" to be alive, Deane said, thanking "Providence for their deliverance."

That joy, however, was undoubtedly short-lived, if not instantly fleeting.

They attempted to find shelter, but there was none of any kind on the barren isle. They were able to create a makeshift tent from remnants of the sail, but through it the "bitter winds of late December whistled and blew, swirling the snow across the icy ledges," Snow writes. Just as starkly, there was no dry wood on the island, so "fire they had none"— for means of a signal, or, just as importantly, for warmth.

Paltry washes of wreckage yielded meager bits of cheese and beef bones. Much of the rest of the ship quickly washed away in the bitter winds and surf.

And, while the men could see vessels going about their maritime business several miles southeast in Portsmouth Harbor, their frantic signals were futile. To increase their chances for rescue, they placed a piece of cloth in the form of a flag atop their tent.

Growing weaker from the ordeal, the elements, and a lack of food, they picked about on the island and gathered what they could for sustenance: mussels, shellfish, seaweed. Their only water? The melting snow around them.

In a rather brutal bout of irony, the ship's cook was the first to succumb to the situation and the elements; he had fallen ill before the wreck, and died on the second day. As Deane gruesomely remembered, "None mentioned eating him, though several, with myself, afterward acknowledged that they had thoughts of it."

It wasn't long before the survivors became gaunt, weak, eyes hollowed and empty, clothes and flesh hanging from their frozen and exhausted bones. They huddled together for warmth, but that didn't prevent frostbite from gnawing away at their fingers and toes; their hands and feet were numb, their skin beginning to discolor, and when they removed their shoes, their skin and nails pulled off with them, to their disgust and horror.

Meanwhile, their tent was so confined that when all were inside, they had to lie back to back, and could only turn over in unison.

Ultimately, there was nothing they could do but deal with the bitter agony and roaring pain as their extremities began to turn black and fall off.

As the days turned into weeks, who can describe their desperation and despair? How many began to court insanity on that isolated isle, or hallucinate on account of malnutrition? How many wished they had surrendered a quick death to the sea, rather than enduring this slow, torturous anguish as they literally became ghosts?

A few of their number, frenzied in their isolation, managed to craft a crude boat—so crude that almost as soon as they attempted to launch it, it was broken up by the roiling surf. They tried once more, and the second time succeeded, but the two men sent off to battle the sea and the elements were never seen by their shipmates again. The body of one washed ashore (eventually prompting a rescue); his companion was never found.

Deane described their resulting lot (while at the same time casting himself as immune and detached): "We were now reduc'd to the most deplorable and mallancholy Circumstances imaginable, almost every Man but myself, weak to an extremity, and near starved with Hunger and Cold; their Hands and Feet frozen and mortified, with large and deep ulcers in their legs (the very smell offensive to those of us, who could creep into the air) and nothing to dress them with, but a Piece of linnen that was cast on shoar."

Finally, completely beyond hope, propelled by the instinct to survive, they resorted to the unthinkable.

At the end of December, after two weeks being stranded, the ship's carpenter succumbed to the cold clawed fingers of death. As Captain Deane later described him, he was "a fat man, naturally of a dull, heavy, phlegmatick (sic) constitution, and aged about 47."

The following morning, the men moved his corpse a distance away from their "camp"—but the enticement of any available kind of meat, even human, was too great.

The starving sailors took a vote: Would they, or would they not, eat the body of their dead shipmate?

The majority agreed.

"After abundance of mature thought and consultation about the lawfullness or sinfullness on the one Hand, and absolute Necessity on the other; Judgement, Conscience . . . were oblig'd to submit to the more prevailing arguments of our craving appetites."

There was no alternative, Deane recalled. So, after "ordering his skin, head, hands, Feet and bowels to be buried in the Sea, and the Body to be quarter'd for Conveniency of drying and carriage," they sliced his body apart, feeding their aching bellies with his raw flesh.

Deane, ever the savior in his own narrative, took on the "task very grievous."

His recipe (of sorts): a few thin slices, wash'd in saltwater, with a good quantity of seaweed in place of bread. The first piece (which he himself ate) was "part of the gristles that compose the breast, having the flesh scrap'd clean off."

He acknowledged that he and others "abominated the loathsome diet," although his "importunate appetite" had led him to the unthinkable, such as surveying "with a longing eye the extremities of his fore fingers."

The mate and two others refused to partake in the flesh-eating that night—but the next morning, constitution completely consumed by hunger, they were the first to "beg an equal share in the common allowance."

The stranded men continued like this for days on end, mutilating the body of their one-time companion.

Then, finally, after twenty-three days on the island, a ship came to their aid on January 2, 1711. A crew from York were there to investigate after the body of one of the raft-makers washed ashore. The rescuers were appalled by what they found: men who were barely stick figures; delirious, frozen, forced by fate into the outright macabre. The survivors were transferred via canoe to a shallop, fed rum and bread, and eventually returned to London, still in shock from their ordeal, many with physical ailments they would live with to their final days.

Deane was quick to publish an account of the wreck that portrayed him as the swarthy hero, recommending it "to the serious perusal of all, but especially sea-faring men."

It soon became a best-seller.

Yet Deane's version of events was quickly refuted, and quite conversely so. The mate Christopher Langman, boatswain Nicholas Mellen, and another of the crew, George White, penned their own account, which charged that the captain was ornery and abusive, once beating Langman with a bottle so severely that he was left for dead. Later, when he recovered and alerted Deane that he was sailing too close to shore, Langman claimed that the captain threatened to shoot him.

The mate also cast Deane as crying and howling for fear of losing his life as the ship went down, and being the one who first proposed eating the carpenter—and wanting to keep the "meat" for himself.

This narrative also attested that four of the *Galley*'s guns were useless, and that only about half the crew had the experience of sailing in unseasonable weather.

Ultimately, the men surmised that the shipwreck was part of an evil master plan: Deane was desperate for the ship's insurance money, so he had intended to betray it to the French, or have it overtaken by pirates, driving it into waters known to be frequented by them. When neither of those attempts worked, they believed he purposely crashed it into Boon. In fact, Langman testified much of this before a justice of the peace before embarking home for England.

Other accounts emerged, as well, and Deane's reputation—and that of his brothers—was ruined. Jasper Deane was said to have died after a fight between the two brothers, and John Deane fled to Russia, where he accepted a commission as a lieutenant in the Russian Navy, and led a successful career capturing ships. He wrote another book on the history of the Russian fleet during the reign of Peter the Great, worked as a spy in St. Petersburg, and served for ten years as consul for the Ports of Flanders at Ostend in Belgium. He spent twenty-three years in retirement before his death in 1761.

But whatever the truth about the *Nottingham Galley* and the crew's torturous time stranded on Boon Island, the pure morbidity of those three weeks left a dark, enduring imprint on the men. To their final days, they had to live with not only lasting physical scars, but the ceaseless chattering of their consciences, vivid memories, and relentless public scrutiny. Even today, 310 years after the fact, we shake our heads in disgust.

Some say the island is forever marked, as well: Visitors claim to have encountered ghosts of emaciated, expressionless sailors; others have heard anguished sighs and lurching footfalls with no origin, or described the intense and unmistakable feeling of being watched.

The wreck lives on in more tangible ways, as well, including a highly-popular fictionalized version, *Boon Island*, penned by Kenneth Roberts in 1956, and a more recent nonfiction account, *Boon Island: A True Story of Mutiny, Shipwreck, and Cannibalism* by Andrew Vietze and Stephen Erickson published in 2012.

Meanwhile, centuries later, small iron cannons, cannonballs, musket shot, and grenades believed to be from the ship have been recovered off the shores of Boon Island—where the lighthouse, and the legends, still stand.

Love, Washed Away

Dress crumpled and streaked with blood, hair tangled and snarled, eyes swollen and red and exhausted of tears, the young woman climbed the winding stairs with pained, halting steps.

At the top, she dragged herself into the small lantern room. Moving with routine, mechanical gestures that seemed led by the hands of another, she cut the wicks on the lanterns and then refilled them with oil.

She took a second to glance out over the ocean: It was a vast, black nothingness indiscernible from the equally dark sky.

Then she descended the tower's 168 steps—to her beloved.

He lay in a heap at the base of the stairs, his body, having been overtaken and then tossed about by the cruel sea, stiffening and decaying.

She resumed her spot beside his frozen corpse, listening to the wind screeching and battering the granite structure, begging to be let in. She didn't want to eat, didn't want to sleep; she just wanted her dear Lucas back.

When they found Katherine Bright nearly a week later, she was on the edge of hypothermia, starved, babbling, and incoherent, cradling her lover's limp body.

Guided by duty, she had kept Boon Island's guiding light burning for five days during a battering storm after her husband had perished in the grip of the ocean's frigid waters.

But exhaustion and grief finally took over and the untended light waned, then died out.

Local fishermen came to investigate, only to find a grisly, heartbreaking sight.

They quickly shuttled the delirious widow and her husband's corpse back to the mainland. It was said that Katherine went mad and died in a hospital soon thereafter.

Her heart-rending story begins in the mid-1800s—it was then that young lighthouse keeper Lucas Bright (name seemingly all too fitting for his profession) brought her to live with him at his station at Boon Island.

Initially, they were happy, spending a pleasant four months keeping house, tending to the lights, and enjoying the ocean air and each other's company.

But then winter set in—a dread for many a New Englander, but especially punishing for lighthouse keepers.

One evening, a particularly unpleasant gale roared over the coast. Lucas, fearing for the island's only boat and frantic to keep the light going, set out into the storm, despite his wife's pleas. As a means of safety, he tied himself to the lighthouse, gave Katherine a kiss, and braced himself against the battering winds and spraying surf.

But as Katherine watched helpless, he was overtaken by a giant wave; it swept up over the island and dragged him into the icy sea, drowning him and smashing his lifeless body against the ragged rocks. Summoning her strength, Katherine hauled and hefted her husband's body in, fighting against the inexorable pull of the sea. She dragged him to the lighthouse, collapsing with him at the base of the stairs—heartbroken, terrified, alone.

But lighthouse keepers are known for their sheer devotion and commitment. Despite her anguish, feelings of helplessness, deteriorating physical and mental state—not to mention the inevitable shock—she knew she had to keep the light going so that others would not suffer the same horrible fate.

Surviving on nothing but will, every few hours Katherine dutifully climbed over her husband's body and up the tower stairs to ensure the lights kept burning. Otherwise, she never left Lucas's side—despite the fact that his body was mangled, frozen and discolored, and rigor mortis was setting in.

She continued like this for five days, until the fuel was nearly diminished and she became too weak to climb the stairs. As she lay beside her husband's body, close to death herself, the light slowly dimmed, flickered, then flared out.

With the tower plunged in darkness, temperatures plummeted, eventually dropping below zero. One can only wonder at the young widow's thoughts in that pitch black, frozen, howling madness. It must have seemed endless and blinding, hope and feeling snuffed out with the light.

But all storms come to an end. When this one ceded to calmer fronts, concerned fishermen from York landed on the island and were shocked to find the incapacitated woman clinging desperately to a corpse.

Her sorrowful end was described in the poem "The Watch of Boon Island" by nineteenth-century poet Celia Laighton Thaxter:

> *They found her watching, silent, by her dead,*
> *A shadowy woman, who nor wept, nor wailed,*
> *But answered what they spake, till all was said.*
>
> *They bore the dead and living both away.*
> *With anguish time seemed powerless to destroy*
> *She turned, and backward gazed across the bay,*
> *Lost in the sad sea lay her rose of joy.*

3

A GRAND DESIGN
THWARTED

"Man marks the earth with ruin; his control stops with
the shore."

—Lord Byron

The mid-1700s were anything but prosperous throughout much of
Ireland.

Disease, poverty, and starvation were rampant due to a prolonged
cold period—what some historians and climatologists have deemed
a mini "Ice Age"—that decimated crops and froze waterways, notably the 224-mile River Shannon (the country's longest river). An
estimated 15 to 20 percent of the population died during this Irish
Famine, a plight that was exacerbated by religious persecution of Pres-
byterians by Catholics, not to mention relentless wars between Britain,
France, and Spain.

Protestants, in particular, suffered from a British hierarchy that
forbade them to own land, hold public office, or marry outside the
Catholic Church.

Many families were desperate, on the brink.

But a shiny hope had begun to emerge: The Colonies of the New World across the Atlantic offered acceptance and new beginnings. It was with this belief—and a "grand design"—that some 200 passengers secured travel on the two-masted bark *Martha and Eliza.*

They never could have imagined that what was to come would rival the many hardships they had already endured.

The 90-foot ship sailed from North Londonderry, Ireland, on July 28, 1741, commanded by Captain Matthew Rowan and headed for the Newcastle, Pennsylvania, settlement nestled on the Delaware River.

Due to trade restrictions and rampant piracy and privateering, the cost of passage was hefty. Many of the passengers on board were people of great wealth and distinction, and they brought with them prized family heirlooms, antiques, fine clothing and linens, as well as male and female bond-servants who traded their freedom for the cost of the voyage.

According to historians, extreme discretion and secrecy amidst this wartime, political, and religious backdrop is also the reason that no passenger list exists.

The Atlantic is a tempestuous force, and the ocean quickly worked its will on the intrepid ship. Four weeks into the journey, a hurricane ripped the masts from the *Martha and Eliza*, and she drifted prone and directionless for several weeks.

Many passengers fell ill; all were starving and an unknown number died.

Finally, after ten weeks Captain Rowan and his crew sighted the faint, dim outline of land in late autumn. Many historical records over the centuries have reported that land to be Mount Desert Island, but new details—from modern Maine historian and folk artist Julia Lane— indicate it that actually could have been Grand Manan Island or White Head Island, situated in the archipelago at the boundary between the Gulf of Maine and the Bay of Fundy.

In any case, it was described as an island with sand beaches and high cliffs—hardly a unique identifier in New England standards—and, ulti- mately, extremely far off course from their intended destination, where passengers' expectant family and friends waited.

While Rowan was said to have experienced further troubles maneuvering the ship to a safe, sheltered harbor—historian Edward Rowe Snow noted that, as he approached land, a southeast gale "caught the ship and pusher her by the Thumper," thus smashing her against "the nubbles." Fortunately, the bedraggled passengers were able to reach the shore of the uninhabited island.

This was purportedly when Rowan revealed his true scoundrel self.

Once the passengers were ashore, he and his crew sailed off with the promise of securing a rescue party and, just as importantly, food and water. But he apparently had no intention of finding either. Instead, he sailed into Fort Frederick at Pemaquid, where he and his men remained for several weeks, gorging themselves on food and drink.

Meanwhile, abandoned without any provisions, the shipwrecked remainder were forced to erect crude shelters from boat remnants, and subsist mostly on seaweed, algae, and the occasional scrounged-for meat of local clams and mussels. The island had no known native mammals to hunt, and migratory birds were scarce as winter approached.

As days turned into weeks, the ill-prepared passengers became ever more faint and exhausted. They started to succumb to weakness, starvation, and dehydration.

As those who ultimately survived would later report in an appeal to the governor of Massachusetts Bay Colony: "In brief, many died at sea and many after we came to land, the corps of which lie . . . on the shore, (because) through weakness we were not able to interr them."

Desperate, a group of several dozen men left for the mainland to find help. But they were never seen again; absconded, attacked by natives, shipwrecked, or stranded once more—their fate remains unknown.

With their departure, the remaining group of mostly women were left alone. And prone.

What meager food and shelter they could round up was said to be stolen by hostile natives, who raided the camp, exploiting women and children without the proper means to defend themselves. According to one account, a family hung a few pieces of their fine clothing in a tree to provide a measure of shelter; but a greedy native ripped the garments free and rushed at the survivors with a tomahawk when they dared protest. In other instances, they made paltry, one-sided trades with the few earthly possessions they had left, typically clothing.

Finally, Captain Rowan returned—but he brought with him two empty shallops and no food. As the starving group watched helplessly, he quickly set to plundering the disabled *Martha and Eliza*, loading his vessels until they bobbed heavily in the water.

Then he did approach the stragglers, offering to take them back to land—but only if they turned over whatever money or possessions they had, or agreed to become bonded servants, as payment for their rescue. Despite the terms, forty-eight accepted, relinquishing all of their belongings, even their clothing, so as "to leave us almost naked."

That group was brought to St. George, one of the many scraggly claws of land extending out into the Atlantic from the Midcoast. There, welcoming settlers also hailing from Northern Ireland, took them in, and appealed to provincial officials, informing them of Rowan's treatment and seeking reparations. The Massachusetts Bay Colony duly reported that 250 pounds were spent for "sundry provisions sent in County Sloop to the poor sufferers that were cast ashore."

Still, several remained shipwrecked on the isle—a group that Snow described as a "pitiful group of women."

Among them: a Mrs. Asbell or Isabell Galloway, who had with her a nursing infant. Her husband, before dying of exhaustion, was said to have traded three pieces of fine Irish linen for a duck; he refused to eat any himself, hoping that the meat would provide proper sustenance for his family. And, when he finally succumbed, his "sorrowing and starving wife was obliged to dig her husband's grave and bury him without help," Snow described.

As Mrs. Galloway's own health deteriorated, her attempts at suckling her child became a gruesome act: Blood instead of milk flowed to the baby's emaciated lips.

Yet somehow, she and ten others survived that wretched, barren landscape through the winter.

The following spring, members of the Passamaquoddy tribe came to the island on an annual pilgrimage to tend the graves of their ancestors, as well as to harvest birds' eggs.

Upon their landing, they were shocked to find the handful of women, including Mrs. Galloway, who still had the strength and health to provide the occasional succor for her baby.

Even though these women were from an area ruled by the British crown—and therefore their sworn enemies—tribal members agreed to paddle 100 miles to St. George to deliver letters with their pleas for help.

Finally, mercifully, a group of men arrived from the seaside settlement—just as shocked by the condition and perseverance of the women as the Passamaquoddy had been—and brought the survivors home with them. There, they received what hospitality, shelter, and sustenance the locals could provide. They were happy merely to sleep on floors or in hovels, it was said, and Mrs. Galloway, in particular, was relieved that the locals were of Northern Irish stock.

The roughly sixty survivors of the *Martha and Eliza* wreck eventually dispersed, some making it to Virginia for their long-awaited reunions, others settling in the Massachusetts Bay Colony, and a few even putting down roots in Maine.

This included Mrs. Galloway, who was courted by, and eventually married, Warren farmer Archibald Gamble. It's said that, once her dead husband's brother heard of the nuptials, he was so offended that he demanded his family be given the surviving baby boy. She responded that she would keep the child until he was old enough to decide for himself.

But as ironic fate or mere coincidence would have it—or, simply, because the ocean provided one of the few viable career options of the day and location—that boy, Richard Galloway, lived to teenagerhood, when he became a seaman and was lost at sea at just seventeen.

Of a hardy, resilient stock, Mrs. Isabel Galloway Gamble, for her part, bore seven more children and experienced many other colorful adventures—including purportedly being captured by Native Americans in

1757 after her husband joined Roger's Rangers, a group of woodsmen that fought for the British during the French and Indian War.

Still, despite the ongoing feud with natives brought about by the expansion of the colonies, it's said that she was kind to local tribespeople until her final days. Today, she rests at the Old Warren burial ground set in a crook of the St. George River.

Meanwhile, another survivor, a Mrs. Sarah Porterfield, settled at New Harbor with the husband she married in November 1742, a year-and-a-half after her rescue. More than fifty-five years later, in 1798, Mrs. Porterfield wrote about her experiences on the *Martha and Eliza* and the ensuing shipwreck.

"I am now seventy-six years old," she wrote. "My anchor of hope has been for many years cast within the veil. My faith rests on the Rock of Ages, which the gates of hell can never prevail."

The dastardly Captain Rowan, for his part, was never brought to justice. Some reports have him turning up as a politician in North Carolina thirteen years later.

Then there remains the quizzical nature of the location of the *Martha and Eliza* shipwreck itself—with respected historians on both sides of the Atlantic placing it at Mount Desert Island near modern-day Acadia National Park, while more recent researchers locate it farther north, at Grand Manan on the Canadian border.

The true saviors of this tale, the Passamaquoddy, have but a few surviving ancestors; they have related the origin story that Manan Island was formed when Dawn, the daughter of land and sea, was chased out to the ocean by wolves, then was transformed into a land mass. It has long been the tribe's belief that Dawn's benevolent influence was the reason for the shipwrecked women's survival. Who can ever say for sure? But human will can often be the most divine influence of all.

A Coastal Conundrum

The etymology of "Downeast" is nautical: It was meant to guide sailors "downward and to the east"—that is, in keeping with the prevailing winds. Today, though, it serves as a catchall for the stretch of coastline from the Penobscot Bay to the Canadian border (depending, of course, on whom you ask). The Downeast area has notoriously puzzled unsuspecting sailors, gobbled up or dashed apart many a ship and sent countless seamen to watery graves.

One of the many examples is the *Sarah*, which wrecked off the islands of Jonesport in 1835 when its captain mistook Mount Desert Rock for Moose Peak Light.

More than a dozen men were lost and the tragedy prompted the ballad, "The Loss of the Sarah":

> *Ye Landsman all, now pray draw near,*
> *A lamentation, ye shall year;*
> *A ship was lost on the sea,*
> *It was the Sarah's lot to be.*
> *Thirty and two were the Sarah's crew*
> *And landsmen were all counted too;*
> *Sixteen survived to reach the shore,*
> *Sixteen are lost, they are no more.*

Mount Desert, in particular, is an area with many distinctly beautiful, placid and pristine hills, valleys and hideaways; among those is Fernald Point, near what is known as Flying Mountain, a popular hiking spot, where modern-day trekkers are rewarded with sweeping views brought in on a salty breeze. Explorer Samuel de Champlain called this setting "ile des Monts Deserts" (or island of bare mountains) on account of its marked lack of vegetation.

Beyond its natural charms, the area is a nationally-recognized archaeological site. A dig in the 1970s revealed shell middens (mounds that are essentially ancient domestic waste dumps) that date to around 1000 BCE.

Yet, one of the area's earliest recorded histories is that of a brutal and bloody massacre.

Fernald Point was the site of the first white settlement on the island, populated by Jesuit missionaries and named Saint Saviour Mission. The men were sent by a noblewoman named Marquise de Boucherville in an attempt to establish a French stronghold in the brave new untamed world (what the monarchy hoped would come to be known as New France).

But in 1613, the missionaries were murdered in a vicious surprise attack by a local fisherman who had been hired by the English to prevent French settlement. They came aboard the *Jonas*, attacking with sixty musketeers and fourteen guns, killing the majority of the settlers and capturing the rest (who at first fled, then, fearing starvation, gave themselves up).

But settlement—as is often the case—persevered, and along with it came more and more maritime trade. In turn, shipwrecks and maritime disasters sharply increased.

To aid navigation, the U.S. government appropriated funds for a lighthouse at Bass Harbor Head; it was built in 1858 and is the only lighthouse situated on Mount Desert Island.

A striking sight, it clings precipitously to a flat perch just at the edge of steep rocks that tumble sharply into the Atlantic. This "squat little lighthouse, in white cassock and black cap" sitting "demurely looking off to the sea" as described by Samuel Adams Drake, has been immortalized in many photos and paintings: fringed by blushing sunsets, wispy clouds, or tinged by the last bit of twilight, the flash of its unique red lens a striking highlight against the white of its tower and keeper's house.

Another lighthouse sits roughly six miles offshore at the tiny seaside hamlet of Swan's Island.

Once a Native American stronghold, the isle was chartered by Champlain in 1604, and was later named for Colonel James Swan, an all-around Renaissance man who participated in the Boston Tea Party in 1773.

The light was erected in 1872 at Hockamock Head, an idyllic promontory jutting out into the bay affording keepers an eagle-eye view of shuttling traffic and the changing temper of the sea.

Author Mary Bradford Crowninshield called the lighthouse the "snuggest and prettiest on the coast," and writer Robert Thayer Sterling described it as a "little place out of the wind and storm (where) sailors found restfulness" (which, due to the tumultuous nature of their profession, can be a difficult task).

Farther north, or "way Downeast," Prospect Harbor Light sits on a sliver of land that, from above, appears as a finger scraping the sea. Built in 1850, the thirty-eight-foot-tall tower guards the eastern edge of its namesake harbor.

Then there is nearby Winter Harbor—and the unusual circumstances that led to the building of its beacon in 1857 on Mark Island, a rocky bump in the ocean just a mile from shore.

Located across from Prospect Harbor by land and Bar Harbor by sea, Winter Harbor earned its name from its strange meteorological characteristic: No matter how cold it gets, ice never forms on its waters—thus ships can navigate it all winter long.

This characteristic was, no doubt, an aid to the Harbor Boys, a gang of Revolutionary Army deserters who targeted isolated villages up and down the Maine coast. Their tactic was to attack in the pitch black in unlit boats guided by oarsmen rather than sail, so as to go unheard and unseen. Once ashore, they terrorized towns by plundering and pillaging, raping women, setting fire to homes, boats, and businesses—and brawling with anyone who interfered.

That is, until Winter Harbor's intrepid locals literally turned the tide on the roving deviants.

Learning that the Harbor Boys were in the area and duly alarmed by their terrorizing ways, the townspeople devised a plan: They would lure the attackers away from their village to the menacing rocks surrounding it.

Learning by scout of the night of their approach, they extinguished all lights in town and placed lanterns on the serrated teeth of rocks that stood as guards at the entrance to their harbor.

Easily taking the bait, the Harbor Boys steered straight toward them—then realized, at the last moment, as they saw solitary lanterns illuminating giant imposing boulders, that it had been a ruse.

Not graced with the quality of self-reflection—or, for that matter, the ability to recognize irony as it mocked them—they were said to have instinctively called for help from their would-be victims, their shocked helmsmen at the same time screaming "Row for your lives!"

But it was too late. Their boat was broken to bits upon the rocks.

No one, it seems, can deceive the merciless sea.

4

THE AMERICAN REVOLUTION IN MAINE

VICTORIES AND LOSSES FOR LIBERTY

"War is sweet to those who have no experience of it, but the experienced man trembles exceedingly at heart on its approach."

—Pindar

To the eyes of eighteenth-century settlers, the Machias River and its environs were a sight to behold. Sixty miles long and running through modern-day Washington County in downeast Maine, it was abundant with salt hay and lined with seemingly endless forests of virgin pine trees.

Sensing great opportunity, several settlers relocated from Scarborough in the southern part of Maine to modern-day Machias (which was officially incorporated in 1784).

By 1770, more than eighty families lived in the area, and they had established five active sawmills and begun lumber-trading with Boston and other colonies.

It was off the shores of this idyllic, prosperous settlement that the first naval engagement of the Revolutionary War was waged.

On June 2, 1775, Machias merchant and British sympathizer Ichabod Jones arrived in the port of Machias with two merchant vessels, *Unity* and *Polly*, accompanied by the HMS *Margaretta*, an armed British schooner. Jones had orders from British military generals involved in the relentless, year-long Siege of Boston to carry flour and other goods to the people of Machias in exchange for desperately-needed lumber to build barracks along the Boston shoreline. He was also instructed by British Admiral Samuel Graves to recover guns from the HMS *Halifax*, which, following a prosperous career combatting colonial unrest, had reportedly been intentionally run aground in local waters four months earlier.

But quickly after setting down anchor, Jones and James Moore, the British midshipman placed in command of the *Margaretta*, were met with resistance. Jones refused to sell pork and flour that he had aboard unless he was allowed to load lumber bound for Boston to aid the British cause.

Over the course of the next several days, locals held town meetings over the matter. They first voted against trading with Jones—then, when the *Margaretta*'s guns were turned on the town as a retaliatory measure, they opted to permit trade.

Finally, when Jones began loading his cargo and declared that he would only trade with those townspeople who had voted in favor of it, many became incensed. Led by Benjamin Foster, local militiamen began conspiring.

Their plan was to capture Jones, but upon hearing rumors of this hostage-taking, Jones fled into the woods. Moore escaped to his boat, raised anchor, and attempted to conceal his fleet a league downstream behind the shelter of a high bank. There, he began to mount more than a dozen short, thick cannons and a handful of larger cannons.

Meanwhile, word had spread, and defiant groups from other settlements started to arrive with guns, pitchforks, and scythes. Two young women who lived along the Chandler River even gathered up roughly forty pounds of lead for musket bullets, then tied all this into a pillowcase and carried it several miles to Machias.

All told, local militia quickly gathered up a "wall piece" (a musket so robust that it had to be rested on a sturdy surface such as a stone wall before it could be fired), more than a dozen guns, several charges of powder, pitchforks, axes, and other implements of destruction.

A group of about thirty local men boarded and easily captured the *Unity*. After bolstering it with makeshift protective structures, they elected Jeremiah O'Brien as their captain and sailed out to take on the *Margaretta*.

In her flight, the enemy ship was forced into brisk winds, where she lost her boom and gaff. Although Moore was able to capture a merchant schooner, taking her captain captive and seizing its spar and gaff, the *Unity* continued to bear down, closing the distance across the bay.

Soon, there was a furious exchange of cannon balls, bullets, the wall piece, and muskets. During the skirmish, the *Unity* was able to pull alongside the *Margaretta*, and the two vessels became locked; O'Brien and his men jumped aboard the British warship, where they dodged musket fire and grenades.

Amidst the cacophony of smoke, explosions, and tangled bodies, Moore was wounded by a musket shot to the chest. With their captain down, the British men grew fearful and disorganized, and surrender came quickly.

The triumphant local forces sailed the *Margaretta* back to Machias, and the spoils of war included two wall pieces, dozens of cutlasses, boarding axes, hand grenades, muskets, and pistols, as well as an ample supply of powder and shot.

Moore, gravely wounded, succumbed the following day. All told, British losses were estimated at more than 100 (although it's important to remember that this number was circulated by locals, and likely inflated with every telling). Rebel forces, meanwhile, reported just two casualties and three injuries.

A definitive American victory, indeed, for what some have since dubbed the "Lexington of the Sea."

Still, history almost always has its asterisks. A well-circulated version of this story has a Liberty Pole as the impetus. Shortly after the battles of Lexington and Concord in April 1775, locals unanimously voted to erect a tall pine-tree pole to pledge their allegiance to the rebel American cause.

But, so it's said, once Moore disembarked the *Margaretta* and witnessed the treasonous sight, he demanded it come down, or else he would be forced to train the guns of his ship on the town and cannonade them.

When the townspeople refused, the battle commenced.

That story also has Ichabod Jones with his fiancé aboard the *Unity*, not to mention numerous personal and household items that he planned to unload. This, some posit, would explain the swift overtaking of the *Unity*.

In any case, in the aftermath, Machias fully expected British retaliation, so they petitioned the Massachusetts Provincial Congress for guidance and assistance. O'Brien and Foster outfitted one of the captured vessels, which they renamed *Machias Liberty*, with breastwork, guns, and swivels.

In July 1775, the ship easily captured two armed British schooners, *Diligent* and *Tatamagouche,* and O'Brien and Foster were formally recognized by the Provincial Congress. *Machias Liberty* and *Diligent* were then commissioned into the Massachusetts Navy with O'Brien as their commander.

A City Aflame

The worst, though, was yet to come. True retaliation came on October 18, 1775, with the infamous Burning of Falmouth.

Captain Henry Mowat led a fleet of Royal Navy vessels to what was then the town of Falmouth, Massachusetts (present-day Portland,

Maine—not to be confused with the city of Falmouth just a few miles north). The notoriously sour-faced and embittered captain had been ordered to "lay waste, burn and destroy" seaport towns that were "accessible to his Majesty's ships . . . and particularly Machias."

Commanding the sixteen-gun HMS *Canceaux*, Mowat anchored his fleet, and then sent a lieutenant ashore to inform residents that they were to receive "a just punishment" for their state of rebellion. They had two hours to evacuate.

Townspeople made a futile gesture for mercy; it was met with a proclamation that Mowat would withhold fire if the town swore an oath of allegiance to King George, and that all small arms, powder, and gun frames and mounts be surrendered.

Faced with an impossible ultimatum, the town was soon emptied, and at 9:40 a.m., Mowat began his bombardment.

As one witness recalled: "The firing began from all the vessels with all possible briskness, discharging on all parts of the town . . . a horrible shower of balls from three to nine pounds weight, bombs, carcasses (incendiary bombs and shells), live shells, grapeshot and musketballs."

The onslaught lasted for nearly nine hours.

Apparently still not satisfied, and clearly out for more than revenge, Mowat sent a group into town to set fire to any buildings that remained standing. While locals did provide some resistance, purportedly killing and wounding some of their attackers, the damage was done: Mowat triumphantly reported that "the body of the town was in one flame."

The British commander attempted to continue his pitiless siege in Boothbay, where he and his men set fire to some houses and raided livestock, but his ships were ailing and winter was descending, so he soon returned to Boston.

But the town of Falmouth was decimated. Although there were no reported deaths, more than 400 buildings and businesses were destroyed, and upwards of 1,000 people were left homeless. It was not until more than twenty years later that significant rebuilding was completed, and reparations in the way of tracts of land were granted by Congress.

And it was not the last encounter Maine would have with the cruel Mowat—or the end of her losses throughout the Revolution.

In fact, Maine served as a significant backdrop to an oft-overlooked mid-war battle (the overlooking undoubtedly due largely to not only the remote location, but the resultant defeat).

The twenty-day assault of Castine in 1779 would serve as the largest American naval expedition in the Revolutionary War, when battles and skirmishes were largely waged on land.

What's more, the Penobscot Expedition, as it was deemed, would go down in history as the U.S.'s worst naval defeat in a single engagement until the infamy of Pearl Harbor during World War II.

The Disastrous Penobscot Expedition

As Britain continued to grapple with what it considered insolent and disobedient colonies, it also clandestinely attempted to establish strongholds and reclaim remote and isolated areas.

Among these was modern-day Castine, snug on the midcoast between Belfast and Mount Desert.

This area bore the native name "Matchebiguatus"—or "a place with no safe harbor"—which perhaps should have been heeded by both British and Colonial forces alike.

Nevertheless, in June 1779, British Brigadier General Francis McLean landed in the area with over 700 men. His task: to build Fort George, gain control over what was then far northern Massachusetts, and establish New Ireland, which would serve as a Loyalist haven, a strategic naval base, a coastal trading post, and provide a steady source of timber for the King's Navy.

Arriving in a flotilla from Halifax, Nova Scotia, McLean was accompanied in this duty by Captain Henry Mowat (infamous for orchestrating the merciless, ruinous Burning of Falmouth). Mowat commanded three British sloops of war—the flagship of which was the HMS *Albany*—anchoring them at the peninsula near the mouth of the Penobscot River.

As McLean later recalled, when the British arrived and asserted dominance, some local families expectedly fled, but others willingly signed oaths of loyalty to King George III. He contemptuously reported that the "misery of the people" in the vicinity was "hardly to be express'd"—in other words, they were not being taken care of by the provincial government, and ongoing blockades, embargoes, and trade restrictions up and down the coast had stymied business, impacting not only their livelihoods but their health and wellbeing.

So, with little initial resistance, the British set to their task.

It wasn't long, though, before the news of their landing and subsequent actions reached the Massachusetts General Assembly in Boston. Not surprisingly, the body was alarmed and incensed, and quickly mounted the Penobscot Expedition (also sometimes referred to as the Bagaduce expedition). The Bagaduce and Penobscot rivers carve parallel paths to the Penobscot Bay, their coursing waters separated by the stubby arrow of land that is Castine.

In July 1779, nineteen armed vessels and twenty-four transport ships made their way up the coast of Maine to execute their ill-fated mission. They carried nearly 350 guns, a land force of 1,200 men, as well as roughly 800 mariners—many of them privateers who helmed ships with names the likes of *Defence*, *Revenge*, *Vengeance*, *Black Prince*, and *Tyrannicide*. The largest vessel in the armada was the thirty-two-gun *Warren* of the Continental Navy.

Commodore Dudley Saltonstall—who had established himself as a skilled commander prior to and during the Revolution, and was intimately familiar with the Castine waters and coastline—led the naval mission. Land forces, meanwhile, were under the command of General Solomon Lovell, who in contrast to Saltonstall, was relatively inexperienced; his most significant prior campaign was a failed attempt to drive the British from Rhode Island in 1776. Notably, Lieutenant Colonel Paul Revere, whose name would become synonymous with American independence, was in charge of the Penobscot Expedition artillery.

Yet while the Americans were confident in their superior numbers, several neglected factors in the haste of assembling the campaign likely doomed it from the start.

First, General George Washington, commander in chief of the Continental Army, was never informed of the operation. Second and more significantly, Massachusetts legislators failed to appoint a Supreme Commander; thus, Saltonstall, Lovell, and Revere were in constant conflict in their strategizing throughout the twenty-day ordeal. Not to mention the fact that the British, thanks to a network of Loyalists, were well aware of—and prepared for—the Americans' arrival.

On July 25, after picking up Penobscot tribesmen and other local sympathizers, the American commanders approached the Bagaduce Peninsula.

The British, for their part, were well underway with construction of Fort George—over which a British flag flagrantly flew—and had constructed three smaller batteries in the harbor and anchored three sloops of war at its entrance.

Two weeks of brief, yet often intense, forays ensued.

American forces attempted to dislodge British ships from their defensive positions with fast attack and retreat moves, but they were met with barrages of fire from sloops and batteries. Lovell's land troops were easily repelled when attempting at least two shore landings.

Finally, a contingent of marines overtook one battery, quickly building a breastwork and firing at British ships, wounding some aboard the *Albany*.

Then, beginning at midnight on July 27, Lovell's land troops gained ground: 1,100 troops landed at Bagaduce Bluff, ascending the steep cliff in dense fog under covering fire from American ships.

Lovell would later write that he was "struck with admiration" to see the precipice that his men had ascended. "It is at least . . . three hundred feet high, and almost perpendicular, and the men were obliged to pull themselves by the twigs and trees."

With Americans out in the open on the cliff face and vulnerable to attack, there were several casualties. But the British also suffered numerous losses.

Lovell's men quickly took cover on the mainland and built a battery within a quarter-mile of Fort George. Meanwhile, British and American ships exchanged heavy fire, and the *Warren*'s masts and rigging were damaged.

Yet despite gains on both sides, the standoff continued.

The Americans awaited word and further orders from Boston; the British sent for reinforcements from New York.

Blessed with 20/20 hindsight, historians have concluded the rationalizing mindsets of commanders on both sides. British General McLean was operating under the belief that the number of troops equaled the size of the formidable American armada; thus, his conservative strategy was to cannonade and launch light infantry.

Similarly, Lovell feared that his force too small; to avoid a large-scale assault, he dug in and also stuck with cannonading and skirmishing. While Saltonstall boasted superior naval strength, outnumbering the British's three-ship defense eight to one, he feared that his largely square-rigged fleet would be unable to maneuver swiftly enough should it enter the harbor. Some also posit that, because much of his fleet was chartered from wealthy and influential Boston merchants and politicians, he feared damaging these vessels far more than suffering a military loss.

In any case, fate was decided on August 12—sixteen days following the American's arrival—when a squadron of British ships began gathering at nearby Monhegan Island. These included the 64-gun ship *Raisonable* and several other heavily-armed frigates. Answering McLean's pleas for additional troops, the fleet had left New York on August 3 under the command of Commodore George Collier.

Two days later, on August 14, Saltonstall appeared to be readying for battle with the now expanded British presence. But, to the surprise of all—his fellow commanders included—he promptly raised sail, turned his ships about, and fled up the Penobscot River. With no further course of action but retreat, he led his fleet farther and farther upriver, the British fast in pursuit. Finally, acknowledging defeat, and hoping to prevent British forces from seizing his ships and weapons and capturing his men, Saltonstall ordered that crews abandon their vessels, take what they could—and destroy all else.

Cacophony ensued: Americans trashed, set fire to, and deliberately sunk (or scuttled) their ships, including the once majestic *Warren*. Many then ran into the forest, spending nights without food or shelter and making the 250-mile overland journey south to Massachusetts.

As Lovell later lamented of the scene, it was "as much confusion as can possibly be conceived."

"To attempt to give a description of this terrible day is out of my power," he recalled. "It would be a fit subject for some masterly hand to describe it in its true colours; to see four ships pursuing seventeen sail of armed vessels, nine of which were stout ships . . . transports on fire . . . men of war blowing up provisions of all kinds, and every kind of stores on shore"

All told, a staggering thirty American ships were destroyed by their own crews.

The British seized roughly a dozen smaller vessels, and also salvaged fifty or sixty cannons that were soon installed at Fort George or transported to Halifax.

The Americans were said to have suffered close to 500 casualties, while the British loss was estimated at just seventy. Due to the rampant damage, the monetary loss to the Revolutionary cause will never truly be known, although estimates put it at $7 to 8 million.

In the days following defeat, local residents fled, leaving many areas largely unpopulated until the end of the Revolutionary War and the signing of a peace treaty.

An ensuing Massachusetts court of inquiry deemed that the primary reason for the defeat was "the want of proper spirit and energy in the commander." Saltonstall and Revere were court-martialed and charged with cowardice and subordination. Determined to be the one primarily responsible for the ordeal, Saltonstall was ultimately dismissed from military service. Revere was also dismissed from the militia, but was later cleared of charges.

The British occupied Fort George until 1783. A year prior, as if harkening the war's outcome, their victorious ship, the *Albany*, was declared unfit for battle and demoted to a prison sloop. After discharging prisoners in Boston, she was wrecked and sunk near Penobscot—and as if a solemn reminder of her duty, her rotting hulk was visible for many years during low tide.

Similarly, the sunken American ships were not all completely lost; for centuries, they have provided visible remnants of history. Most notably, in the 1970s, a team from the Maine Maritime Academy and the Massachusetts Institute of Technology applied sonar methods to locate the remains of the *Defence* off Sears Island. Much of her hull remained intact, and over the years, more than 2,000 artifacts were excavated from her depths—cannons, cannonballs, grapeshot remnants, a copper cauldron, pewter spoons, navigational instruments, small medicine chests, and a whistle crafted from bone. These items are now in the possession of the Maine State Museum.

The Penobscot River and Bay have similarly yielded cannons, an eighteenth-century cast-iron swivel gun, silver coins, brass shoe buckles, tobacco pipes, pocketknives, and hundreds of pieces of ceramic glass and brick—all thought to be from the destroyed ships.

All of this, perhaps, serves as a reminder that history can always be unearthed.

The epilogue to this story comes during the War of 1812, when the British once again attempted to establish a New Ireland colony. In August 1814, Sir John Sherbrooke led a British force from Halifax, and Castine was retaken.

Meanwhile, British Captain Robert Barrie defeated a local militia and sunk an American frigate, to make Mainers pay for their previous "crimes" during the Revolutionary War. His troops also sacked Hampden on the Penobscot River—they burned, smashed, and looted whatever they could.

When the locals begged Barrie to show humanity, his response was ruthless and brutal: "Humanity! I have none for you. My business is to burn, sink, and destroy. Your town is taken by storm. By the rules of war we ought to lay your village in ashes, and put its inhabitants to the sword. But I will spare your lives, though I mean to burn your houses."

Those words would forever remain etched in the minds of those who heard them—and, centuries later they serve as a harsh reminder that there are no rules in war, whether waged on land or sea.

5

PERILOUS PORTLAND
WATERS

"Chaos was the law of nature; order was the dream of
man."

—Henry Adams

It is an iconic capturing of a ship's demise—and arguably one of the
most widely-circulated images in modern maritime history.

A three-masted vessel, stripped of its sails, lilts sideways, propped
up on sharp, jagged rocks not far offshore from a majestic lighthouse.
Morose, forlorn, crippled, the *Annie C. Maguire* rests upon the ledge
that permanently grounded her in late 1886.

The notorious wreck is further memorialized with a simple epitaph
painted on a rock below the sidewall of the light tower, first set down in
stark black and white by Joseph Strout: "In memory of the ship *Annie
C. Maguire* wrecked here, Dec. 24, 1886."

Bound from Buenos Aires, she is one of the countless number of
wrecks that have occurred in the perilous, fickle, rock-strewn waters
around Portland—and one that the lighthouse, despite keeping a ceaseless watch, could not prevent.

It is impossible to talk about Maine maritime history—and its unfortunate legacy of shipwrecks—without including (and heavily emphasizing) Portland Head Light. Commissioned by George Washington, the state's first lighthouse was built in 1791, and it continues to be one of Maine's most visited landmarks. With its white tower and red-shingled outbuildings, the lighthouse stands guard on the craggy precipice of the Atlantic, rocks just below appearing like layers of petrified wood in their thousands of years enduring the blows and caresses of the sea. Just offshore, hundreds of boulders of all sizes jut up from the turbulent waves or hide just below the surface, including, most notoriously, Alden's Rock.

An archetypical emblem, the light tower has been immortalized in prose by Henry Wadsworth Longfellow and Harriet Beecher Stowe, not to mention millions of images: splashed by the dull morning rays of the sun, dyed a myriad of hues in sunset, swathed in mist, dusted with snow, flanked by spring flowers, bracing itself against probing waves as the rocks below it are temporarily swallowed by the sea. Today it is owned by the town of Cape Elizabeth, and it sits adjacent to the ninety-acre Fort Williams Park—whose practice fire it bore the brunt of for a time—an idyllic setting that attracts hundreds of thousands of visitors a year.

But this iconic lighthouse was a reactionary measure to disaster.

Between 1780 and 1990, some 100 vessels were estimated to have wrecked upon the Cape Elizabeth coast, and the locale has long been said to have a superstitious aura for mariners.

One example of the area's treacherous waters occurred on June 26, 1863, when the Civil War's northernmost naval battle was waged just off its shores. Under the cloak of night, Confederate lieutenant Charles W. Read and his crew snuck into Portland and boarded the well-armed U.S. cutter the *Caleb Cushing*. They intended to sail it out of port and then turn it back on the city.

But not long after commandeering the ship, they were betrayed by the harbor's boisterous tides—and were thus easily overtaken and captured by Portland forces.

Locals long clamored for a lighthouse on Cape Elizabeth, growing particularly agitated in February 1787. It was then that a 90-ton sloop heading south from Sheepscott on the midcoast wrecked on Cushing Island (located about a mile from where Portland Head Light now stands). The captain and a young boy drowned; the remainder of the crew escaped on floating wreckage.

The following week, *The Cumberland Gazette* demanded, "Does not this unhappy accident evidence the necessity of having a Lighthouse at the entrance of the harbor?"

The light was eventually commissioned by Washington before either the federal government or Maine existed (the state would remain part of Massachusetts until 1820), and was constructed partly of local rubblestone.

But as we shall read, Portland Head couldn't quell all catastrophe.

The Blight of the *Bohemian*

In February 1864, the *Bohemian*, having made the long ocean trek from Liverpool, England, broke apart upon the rocks below the Portland Head's craggy overlook.

The 2,200-ton ship had been built in 1859 in Scotland, and made runs in the summer between Liverpool and Quebec and in the winter between Liverpool and Portland under the operation of the Montreal Ocean Steamship Company.

With a crew of ninety-nine and a passenger list of 219, the *Bohemian* was captained by Robert Borland. The majority of her passengers were Irish immigrants traveling steerage; the ship also had nineteen cabin-class passengers, and it was said to be carrying a cargo of expensive silks and other fine goods (which some have valued at around $1 million).

Stormy weather delayed the vessel several days and the transatlantic voyage was slow. It was late on the afternoon of February 22 that the *Bohemian* arrived at Cape Elizabeth.

And, in that manner, rather abruptly.

Borland had been making transatlantic runs for the Montreal company for eight years, and was intimately familiar with the waters around Portland. Thus, it was said that a "peculiar condition of haze" confused him into thinking that he was quite a distance offshore—when in actuality, he was only about two miles from Cape Elizabeth and dangerously close to Alden's Rock.

The notorious outcropping serves as the apex of a mile-long submerged ledge; in high water and heavy weather, it is often completely washed over, while at low water, it rises to within just four feet of the surface.

Long considered a navigational hazard, Alden's Rock was first marked in 1835 by a red buoy that extended twenty feet above water and was topped with a flag on a 12-foot-tall staff. Twenty years later, that marker was replaced with a 500-pound bell mounted atop a thirty-foot-long black iron boat emblazoned with "Alden's Rock." Four years later, the boat-and-bell marker were removed and replaced with a conventional buoy. This marker should have warned Borland and his crew of the *Bohemian*'s mortal position. But once it was sighted—and very close ahead—it was too late.

Borland immediately ordered the *Bohemian*'s speed be reduced to a knot and a half (in maritime terms, little more than drifting) to attempt to quell the force of impact.

But the *Bohemian* inevitably smashed into, then slid over, Alden Rock. It was just about 9 p.m.

The crew made quick work of sending up rockets and blue lights while also firing the ship's gun, and Borland ordered full steam of the engines in an attempt to break free of the ledge. But the stubborn rock held the ship strong in its grip, and water rose in the ship's fractured hull. Within ten minutes, the engines stopped. At this point, the ship's port gun was also fully submerged by the frigid Atlantic.

Borland and his crew conceded when they realized that the engine compartment had sprung a terminal leak. In defeat, the captain steered for land, with the ship drifting closer to shore by about two miles until the crew dropped anchor.

By now, frantic passengers—most of whom had been asleep below deck at the time of impact—had rushed topside, where they gathered, shivering and terrified, around the lifeboats. There were six of these dories in total: Three were designed to hold 100 passengers, while the others were at full capacity with just forty.

Keeping his calm despite extreme circumstances, Borland ordered the lifeboats be prepared, loaded, and lowered.

But as his men attempted to maintain order, hysteria grew.

Adding to the growing pandemonium, once the No. 2 lifeboat had been filled with passengers, a pin broke—and everyone was dropped into the sea. As historian Edward Rowe Snow explains, this accident ultimately caused the greatest loss of life during the disaster: With the dory swamped, several passengers were drowned (the exact number is unclear, with reports ranging from sixteen to forty).

When the wrecked lifeboat eventually drifted ashore a few miles away, it was discovered to be a floating coffin for a man and a boy.

Meanwhile, the other five lifeboats were successfully launched. But with their rowers giving in to fear, many of these were only partially filled. As they glided away from the doomed *Bohemian*, those left on board the sinking ship desperately jumped into the water and attempted to climb aboard. Many drowned or quickly froze in the process.

Borland, enraged at this cowardice, immediately ordered the half-filled rescue boats to return to the ship—but their rowers refused, instead paddling away to the safety of land.

The despondent captain, a handful of crewmen, and seventy or eighty passengers were left stranded. As the steamer continued to slowly sink, Borland ordered that everyone move aloft. About fifty women and children were helped into the foretop (the platform at the precipice of the vessel's foremast), while most male passengers and crew climbed into the ship's rigging, ascending higher and higher as she settled into the water.

One passenger, Mary Goham, later described her ordeal of being bound to a mast for hours until she was rescued. Clearly a resilient soul, the native of County Galway, Ireland, lived to be 101—and was, at the time of her death in 1895, the oldest living resident of Lynn, Massachusetts.

The passengers remained stranded, literally hanging on for their lives, as the ship continued to slip into the ocean. Finally, around 10:30 p.m., the *Bohemian* settled in four or five fathoms (25 to 30 feet) of water just about an eighth of a mile from shore.

Then, just before midnight, rescue arrived—the very same lifeboats that had previously fled now mercifully shuttled back from shore.

Borland, perhaps reluctant to leave his ship, was among the last to be removed.

After making the trek to shore to ensure all surviving passengers had made it to safety, he returned once more to his ship in the pre-dawn hours. One of the men accompanying him was Benjamin Willard, a Cape Elizabeth native and harbor pilot. He later wrote of the experience: "When we got to the ship, it was the hardest sight that I had ever looked at." Borland, he lamented, "seemed to be completely prostrated over the loss of his ship and the passengers."

The Portland Advertiser seconded these morose sentiments: "It is hardly necessary to speak of the awful grandeur of the scene," the newspaper printed in one of the many stories that appeared following the wreck (in newspapers and magazines up and down the east coast, as well as back in Ireland).

The New York Times announced the wreck with the blaring (and rather erratic) headline:

SERIOUS MARINE DISASTER.; WRECK OF THE
STEAMSHIP BOHEMIAN. NINETEEN LIVES LOST.
Full List of the Cabin and Steerage Passengers. The Cargo

Valued at One Million Dollars. Capt. Borland's Report upon the Condition of the Vessels. NAMES OF THE LOST. RECOVERY OF MAIL BAGS. Bids for the New Bounty Fund Loan.

That above-mentioned report by Borland testified that the haze had made the land seem many miles farther away than it actually was. His three lookouts attested to this, as well.

And, while he ultimately attempted to reach shore, fires in the quickly-submerging engine room were drowned within minutes, and his "proud ship" went down near Richmond's Island in just ninety minutes after the collision.

The coroner's inquiry ruled that the accident was the result of an error in judgment on Borland's part, the lack of a bell on Alden's Rock, and the inattention of local lifesavers for not noticing the signals from the *Bohemian*.

The fact that it was George Washington's birthday came as an unfortunate coincidence in that last regard: The ship's distress signal and the firing of its gun were interpreted as part of the patriotic festivities occurring up and down the coast.

In all, forty-two perished—all casualties were Irish steerage passengers—and the bodies were recovered by locals, then laid out under sails in the blacksmith house next to the Ocean House hotel. Twelve unclaimed corpses were buried in a mass grave at Calvary Cemetery in South Portland.

This grave remained unmarked until 1984, when two local organizations, the Ancient Order of Hibernians and the Irish American Club of Portland, dedicated a large granite Celtic cross to the men and women lost aboard the *Bohemian*.

Meanwhile, in the days following the tragedy, locals opened their homes to survivors, housing and feeding them. The Portland Board of Trade also collected $1,500 and clothing to distribute among the survivors. Temporary living space was even provided for some of the passengers in Portland's recently-built city hall.

All the while, out in the harbor, the ship proved a sorrowful sight: At low tide, her main deck barely showed above surface, while at high water, only the masts and smokestack were visible.

While nearly three dozen mail sacks aboard were later recovered by divers, most of the other goods aboard floated away with the tides. The majority of this—clothing, boxes of tea, spools of cotton, skeins of valuable silks—soon washed ashore.

Despite the continued vigilance of a shore patrol and a firm notice by steamship agents that forbade anyone to "trawl, fish, seek for, or abduct" any items from the wreck, scavengers appeared day and night, loading everything they could carry into carts and wagons. Armed guards were quickly sent in to protect cargo, and culprits were caught and arrested.

The goods thus recovered by their rightful owners, they were then ferried to Portland and auctioned off—these included carpeting, textiles, silks, broadcloths, cashmeres, tweeds, and linens (some of them still in their original packaging). Elegant bronze fixtures and woodwork were also retrieved from the wreck.

As for the ailing ship itself: The steamship company initially intended to refloat the *Bohemian* and bring her into Portland Harbor. But the Atlantic apparently wasn't done with her yet—a gale blew in several days after the crash and broke the ship apart.

A captain from New Brunswick then set to work dynamiting the broken, sunken hulk to salve more than 1,500 tons of iron. Cannons were pulled up, and divers reported that hundreds of thousands of dollars' worth of property remained in the lowermost hold, which had been protected due to its sides caving in. Because of its location, though, this boon of items was never recovered, and was eventually dragged away by the sea.

Some good did come of the disaster. As a result of the *Bohemian* wreck, the Portland Head Lighthouse was raised by twenty feet. Five months later, in July 1864, $20,000 was appropriated by Congress for those improvements, as well as to provide a better marker at Alden's Rock.

Even so, the precipitous ledge continued to baffle sailors.

One of the many ensuing examples involves the three-masted Canadian schooner *Adelaide*, which went aground at Alden's Rock on December 23, 1886. More than twenty years after the *Bohemian* tragedy, all that marked the deadly Alden's Rock at the time of the *Adelaide*'s crash was a common can buoy—a prime example of man's enduring hubris and folly when it comes to maritime matters.

The Curious Plight of the *Annie C. Maguire*

Yet of the many wrecks at Portland Head over the years, that of the *Annie C. Maguire* in 1886 was one of the most peculiar.

The 188-foot clipper started out its sea life as the *Golden State*, and was launched in January 1853. She was considered one of the fastest and most durable vessels built in the golden age of clipper slips—these being narrow in length, with a large sail area, and built for speed.

And she had quite the career, too. The *Golden State* nearly broke many sailing records; she carried the largest-ever cargo of tea from China to New York in 1867; her crew endured a mutiny in the mid-1850s; and she was involved in the rescue of nine shipwrecked Chinese sailors in 1881. Finally, in 1883, she was sold and renamed, sailing for a few years under the British flag up and down the North and South American coasts.

Then came her fateful—and puzzling—sail and ultimate demise in 1886.

Just a few days before the disaster, a local sheriff paid a visit to Portland Head lighthouse keeper Joshua Strout. During this house call, he foretold of a three-masted schooner headed for Quebec, presented papers on behalf of a Boston bank, and asked Strout to keep an eye out for the vessel, which was slated for seizure by American creditors.

The ship was known to be captained by Thomas O'Neal, and had fifteen members aboard, including O'Neal's wife and twelve-year-old son.

Then, right around 11:30 p.m. on Christmas Eve, a ship bound from Buenos Aires smashed into the ledges off the Cape—hitting so hard that it shook the lighthouse and adjacent keeper's dwelling with the impact.

According to local reports, weather at the time was 46 degrees and it was snowing heavily. Joseph Strout, son of keeper Joshua Strout, told reporters later that "the wind was howling a gale. It was Christmas Eve, you know, and I guess even Santa Claus was afraid to be out." He also attested that, the snow was so heavy that "you couldn't see a hand in front of you," and, eerily, that the "world was as silent as death."

Due to these various conditions, it was believed that O'Neal lost his bearings and wasn't able to make out the silhouette of the lighthouse or its bright light. Either that, or he considered the light tower much farther away than it was. Whatever the reason for the disaster, immediately upon impact, O'Neal ordered his crew to drop sail and lower anchors.

The distressed ship was no more than 100 feet from the tower, plainly visible from land. It made such a rapturous noise that Joshua burst through the door of the keeper's house and exclaimed, "All hands turn out! There's a ship ashore in the dooryard!"

Reacting quickly, keeper Strout—who, it has been said, kept a parrot with the ability to foretell foul weather—and Joseph rigged up emergency lights and began helping passengers to safety.

While the traditional story is that a "breeches buoy," or rope chair, was used to haul the crew to shore one-by-one, a conflicting report has the keeper and his son laying a ladder across the rocks to the ship. Meanwhile, Joseph Strout himself later said that the water was calm enough to permit the men to jump ashore, "almost without help, so hard on the ledge was the vessel (lodged)."

In any case, O'Neal was the last to leave.

And so the story goes, once he was on dry land, he discovered that a satchel that had been on board, holding all of the ship's money and papers, was inexplicably missing. Panicked, he whispered to his wife, who advised that he be quiet and pretend it had been lost. Apparently, she had hidden all of the satchel's contents inside her hatbox.

Although the sheriff did eventually come by to search the ship, the pair absconded with their take. The *Maguire*'s creditors received compensation at auction—but nothing close to the riches that the couple was said to have stolen.

Over the years, it has been suggested that O'Neal purposely wrecked the ship to collect insurance money and throw creditors off his tail. Others have refuted this, saying it was too risky a proposition given that he had his family on board.

More likely, as O'Neal attested himself, the discombobulating weather was the culprit.

And ultimately, Portland's waters never gave up their secrets—the *Maguire* broke apart in a storm not long after the wreck, and now she lives on only in legend.

Tragedy Endures

Of course, not all wrecks in Portland's waters have been as notorious or casualty-laden as these just mentioned—but these lesser disasters are no less significant for the mariners, survivors, and witnesses involved.

Just five years after the *Bohemian* disaster, in early December 1869, the schooner *Mary Alice* struck a reef below Portland Head Light.

The 90-ton vessel was carrying a load of coal from New York. At around 5 p.m., the ship ran into thick weather and blinding snow. As both of these intensified, the captain headed toward lights that he assumed came from the lighthouse—when in actuality, they emanated from the home of John Trundy.

The vessel slammed into the jagged reef at 7:20 p.m., and although the crew attempted to work her free, she rapidly filled and capsized. The cook was immediately drowned; the remaining crewmen managed to hang onto the remnants of the boat, desperately awaiting rescue.

By 2 a.m., captain J.C. Perry—weak, exhausted, and nearly frozen—lost his grip and was washed away. One of his deckhands was also hauled into the sea by the same forceful wave.

As reported in the December 9, 1869, edition of the *New York Herald*, "the crew clung to the vessel, hoping, yet doubting, that succor might come."

Miraculously, they were able to maintain their positions on floating pieces of wreckage until 8 a.m., when they were finally sighted from shore, rescued, and recovered—despite extreme freezing and atrophy.

As reported by the *Herald*, forty-two-year-old Captain Perry left behind a wife and two children, while the cook, twenty-five-year-old Eugene Decrow, left behind a wife and one child. Deckhand Robert C. Pendleton, meanwhile, was an unmarried bachelor. The two survivors were identified as E.T. Achorn and Fred Duncan.

The men aboard the *Susan P. Thurlow* endured a similarly grim fate. On December 16, 1897, the ship was bound from Hillsboro, New York, carrying a cargo of plaster rock. According to the one survivor, E. Reimann, rough weather off the coast battered the boat, and the captain opted to make for Portland Harbor for shelter. He was just a few miles from shore when the rudder rope parted, and the vessel "became disabled and was left at the mercy of the heavy sea," Reimann told the *Daily Times* of New Brunswick.

The captain and crew hastily attempted to repair the steering gear, but, while focused on this task, the schooner struck a reef. All three masts were immediately carried away.

During that impact, a topmast struck the captain and crushed one of his legs. In his dying throes, he ordered the rest of the men to jump for their lives.

Reimann, for his part, was caught by a single wave and hurled into the sea. He recalled being thrown about by the ocean; he washed up on the island three times, but unable to obtain a foothold, he was repeatedly swept back undertow. Weak and choking on seawater, he finally managed to heft his weight onto one of the spars from the destroyed ship. Pushed by the insistent waves, this spar eventually carried him to the beach and saved his life.

As the *Times* reported, "he lay on the beach, benumbed with cold, and exhausted by his battle with the waves, for some time."

Yet the human will is strong: The shipwrecked sailor found the strength to drag himself to the hut of a fisherman. The startled man cared for him until morning, when he brought Reimann to Portland.

Ultimately, the acting captain and five members of the crew were lost; their bodies washed ashore during the night.

The vessel, too, was destroyed. By the morning, there was nothing left of her—the only evidence of her existence was the beach, which was "strewn with spars and other wreckage," according to news reports.

Another of the countless casualties of the ceaseless sea.

6

A SECOND CHANCE
AT REVOLUTION

THE WAR OF 1812 IN MAINE

"Only the dead have seen the end of war."

—Plato

Being the northernmost U.S. territory at the time (and then still part of Massachusetts; statehood would come but a few years later in 1820), Maine didn't see much action in the War of 1812. Many of the campaigns of that erroneously-named war—which actually lasted from 1812 to 1815—were waged farther south.

Yet one instance where Maine's waters served as a set piece for man's battle against himself during what many consider to be America's second revolution occurred not far off the coast of Monhegan Island. It was there that the British vessel HMS *Boxer* and the Yankee ship the USS *Enterprise* vied for domination in the Atlantic's tumultuous waters. The naval combat took place on September 5, 1813, with captains Samuel Blyth of the *Boxer* and William Burrows of the *Enterprise* overseeing the day's bloody events.

Burrows, a native of Philadelphia, had assumed command of the *Enterprise* on August 22, 1813, and was responsible for a strip of coastline along mid-coast Maine that served as open maritime zone—that is, where merchants and privateers British and American alike sailed freely. With a crew of 102, the *Enterprise* was equipped with several carronades (short, large-caliber cannons) and long guns.

Blyth, for his part, had earned a reputation for his attacks and plunders of merchant vessels in Maine waters; yet at the same time, he had been commended for his chivalrous nature and courage. The *Boxer* had 66 men aboard, and an arsenal of carronades and long guns equaling those of the *Enterprise*.

On Sunday, September 5, under a light wind and calm seas, the enemy ships approached one another off the coast of Pemaquid Point.

They maneuvered for several hours until Blyth, who ordered Union Jacks nailed to his ship's foremast and mainmasts, finally fired on the *Enterprise* around 8:30 a.m.

The calm air was suddenly filled with deafening explosions as the *Enterprise* returned fire. The American ship then sailed directly for the *Boxer* and slammed into it broadside.

As residents from the surrounding shores looked on, the ships fired away, cannons sending out consuming clouds of smoke. The *Enterprise* rammed the *Boxer* again. Then once more.

Blyth was killed with the first jarring impact when an 18-pound cast iron cannonball exploded out of one of the *Enterprise*'s guns and struck him in the midsection.

Burrows was hit by a musket ball that tore through his thigh and left him mortally wounded, but still able to order his First Lieutenant to out-sail the *Boxer*, turn, fire on her bow, and smash her once again on her starboard side.

The *Boxer* slipped away before the *Enterprise* could execute this plan, but it was shot dead center by one of her rival's long guns. The British crew immediately ceased firing and called out to surrender.

As is carved into Burrows's gravestone, the battle was a "severe contest of forty-five minutes."

When Blyth's second in command came aboard the *Enterprise* to accept defeat and present Burrows with Blyth's sword as a victory prize, the American captain refused, instead directing that the weapon be sent to the dead man's family. He then purportedly uttered, "I am satisfied, I die contented."

In a morbidly poetic twist, the two young captains—Burrows, 28 and Blythe, 29—lay side-by-side in large box tombs in Portland's Eastern Cemetery. A joint funeral was held for the fallen men on September 9, 1813.

As Burrows's stone proclaims, "A passing stranger has erected this memorial of respect to the memory of a Patriot who in the hour of peril obeyed the loud summons of an injured country, and who gallantly met, fought, and conquered the foeman."

Blyth's tomb, meanwhile, attests: "In life honorable! In death glorious! His country will long deplore one of her bravest sons. His friends long lament one of the best of men."

Two years after the battle, Lieutenant Kervin Waters was buried beside them. Waters had been badly wounded in the fight, and "languished in severe pain which he endured with fortitude" until his death on September 26, 1815. As his inscription reads, it was then that "he died with Christian calmness of resignation."

The brief but bloody battle had a significant impact on many who witnessed it, including a young Henry Wadsworth Longfellow. A Portland native, his prolific pen would be spurred by sea tragedies and triumphs. His uncle, Henry Wadsworth, had served as a "messmate" to Burrows aboard the *Constitution*, and Burrows had been expected to pay a visit to the family while serving in the area.

While Longfellow was only 6-years-old when the battle raged, this melancholy homage is a testament to its lasting impression on him. It also reflected the prevailing sentiment of the day—notably of the loss of two young, valiant men.

I remember the sea fight far away:
How it thundered o'er the tide;

And the dead captains, as they lay
In the graves o'erlooking the tranquil bay
Where they in battle died.
And the sound of that mournful song
Goes through me with a thrill
A boy's will is the wind's will,
And the thoughts of youth are long, long thoughts.

Dashing Into History (and Legend)

It happened in 1942, during the thick of the world's second Great War.

The Allies were performing a routine patrol of the Portland harbor, a key staging port. All was calm and quiet. Fog and thick humidity fell over the area like a shawl.

And then, suddenly, an unmistakable blip appeared on the radar.

Primed for action, all hands were on deck as naval, Coast Guard and British boats descended on a location known as Hussey Sound near Peaks Island.

The radar flashed and beeped; the crewmen reported the faint silhouette of an unknown vessel upon the waves.

And then, as abruptly as it began, everything stopped.

The beeps ceased, the crew paused, and the air was once again still. The sea smoke dissipated to reveal not a wake nor a wave—or any evidence whatsoever that an enemy ship had been in the area. All that the sailors on the imposing convoy of vessels could see was a tiny rowboat adrift in the water carrying two terrified, gape-mouthed illicit lovers staring up at them.

Later, that pair (in the area under the cover of mist for a secret rendezvous) offered their version of events.

Alarmed by the sudden bluster, they recalled that they looked out across the bay to see the battleships fast in pursuit of a curious-looking boat; it was a masted schooner of the Revolutionary days, sails high, hull parting the waves. It passed within yards of them, and, just as it disappeared into the thick fog, they saw that its bow was inscribed with the name *DASH—FREEPORT*.

Like most locals, they knew the story of the fabled privateering ship, which had disappeared beyond Portland Head Light without even a ripple 130 years before under the same sails but amidst a different war.

The *Dash*, the stuff of both legend and romanticism, has been described as Maine's version of Odysseus's fated ship: seemingly bound to ride the seas forever seeking port.

She was built (as her name would suggest) for speed in 1813. The Freeport-based merchant brothers Sewald and Samuel Porter had her crafted especially for smuggling and eluding. She quickly developed a reputation for both; on her first maiden run out of Portland to Santo Domingo, in fact, she crossed courses with an established British brig but easily outraced it. Upon her return, her owners were given permission by President James Madison to hunt British ships as a privateer—a bonus being that she could keep all her spoils. She captured 15 ships without losing a single crew member. Then came her last voyage in early 1815.

Setting sail from Portland, she was met by a new privateer to local waters. Known as the *Champlain* and based out of Portsmouth, New Hampshire, her cocky captain wanted a race.

The *Dash*'s captain, 24-year-old John Porter, was never one to shirk away from such a challenge. So the two set out, very briefly bow to bow. They were last seen passing the Portland Head Light, with the *Dash* in the lead.

However, a tempest blew in and the *Champlain* lost sight of its rival before turning back to port.

And that was where the earthly manifestation of the *Dash* sailed out of this story. She disappeared, leaving no trace of her crew, cargo, or even a scrap of wreckage.

Some say she was cursed, because her captain, in his haughtiness, refused to heed the telltale signs of ill-tidings such as misfiring weapons and bluebirds (said to be harbingers of foul weather).

Nobody knows precisely what became her fate; she could have capsized while her sails were up in full race mode, or she might have been smashed apart on uncharted land.

Whatever her end, the *Dash* was mourned by locals and family members of the crew, who were said to habitually make the climb up to the lantern room of Portland Head Light to keep vigil should she one day return.

A few months later, a fisherman working in the Freeport harbor was suddenly swathed in fog; he was undeterred, however, continuing with his duties.

But then he was shocked to a standstill.

Suddenly, a sailing ship with full mast emerged from the cloaked waters, moving forward despite the fact that there was hardly any wind. On its side, its name stood out in bold letters: *DASH—FREEPORT*.

Since then, the vessel has purportedly been seen sailing all over Casco Bay, off the coast of Freeport, near Harpswell Sound, and around the hundreds of islands splayed along Maine's sizable dominion of the Atlantic.

Some have described her as having tattered sails; others recall seeing her in full regalia of old. In some cases, superstitious sailors and fishermen have sworn to Davy Jones that they witnessed her equipped with a phantom crew standing motionlessly, faces expressionless, on her decks. No matter her condition or whereabouts, it is said that the ship promptly disappears whenever approached, or just as she might collide with land.

Another legendary "phantom ship" said to roam Maine's waters is the *Red Jacket*, a Bath schooner that was first launched in 1854 and disappeared soon thereafter. The schooner was renowned for her speed, having once made a record-breaking cross of the Atlantic. As such, she was said to materialize on still, calm evenings in Portland waters, fast in pursuit. When she finally overtook her rival vessel, there was no crew on her deck, and her sails billowed as if blown by Aeolus despite a lack of any wind.

Then there was the *Whidaw*, a ship said to be captained by renowned pirate Samuel Bellamy. In the heyday of piracy as the New World was spottily being settled, he plundered all over Maine's coast and southeast Canada, eventually establishing a base in what is current-day Machiasport. One day, however, his cockiness got the better of him. The *Whidaw* was damaged when he attacked a French warship in the waters off Nova Scotia. Bellamy then attempted to join forces with a whaling ship out of New Bedford, but he accidentally ran the vessel straight into a sand bank, drowning him and all his crew. Since then, purportedly, the ghost of the *Whidaw* has been seen full-sail in waters all over the Downeast, flying a black flag, forever in pursuit of its next bounty.

As for the *Dash*: Her miserable tale has been memorialized by both Longfellow and Harpswell native son Robert P. Tristram Coffin. Perhaps the most well-known homage, though, is John Greenleaf Whittier's "The Dead Ship of Harpswell," which describes a ship that endlessly prowls the "hundred-harbored Maine":

> *For never comes the ship to port,*
> *Howe'er the breeze may be;*
> *Just when she nears the waiting shore*
> *She drifts again to sea.*
> *No tack of sail, nor turn of helm,*
> *Nor sheer of veering side;*
> *Stern-fore she drives to sea and night,*
> *Against the wind and tide.*

7

THE *ROYAL TAR*

THE GREAT CIRCUS DISASTER

"We are like other animals; we live and die as they do.
If there is any afterlife, I believe we are in together."
—Bangambiki Habyarimana

When the circus vessel, the *Royal Tar*, went down off the coast of Vinalhaven in Penobscot Bay in 1836, it was pure pandemonium—and a maritime tragedy like no other. Men and women flailed about as they were battered by waves, clinging to any bit of wreckage or debris that their exhausted arms could get hold of. Panicked horses swam in circles, whinnying in confusion. Giant cats, camels—even an elephant, thunderously trumpeting and stomping—all fought for their lives in icy, turbulent waters. The centerpiece of all this: a steamer consumed by furious flame, sinking and sending forth black, ashy plumes of smoke that could be seen for miles.

Just a few days prior, the ship's voyage had started out festive, even triumphant.

It was the culmination of a successful, if hectic, touring season for the Macomber, Welch and Company Menagerie. Featuring "Dexter's Locomotive Museum" and "Burgess' Collection of Serpents and Birds," the traveling circus made a three-month, ten-city tour through Canada's maritime provinces.

Its chief attraction: Mogul the elephant. According to the 1841 book by Charles Ellms, *The Tragedy of the Seas*, the pachyderm was quite the celebrity:

> His performances in the ring would scarcely be credited, had they not been daily witnessed by hundreds. A word or a look was sufficient to stimulate him to the greatest exertions. He caressed his master in the best manner, and would not so readily obey another person. He received his orders with attention, and executed them cheerfully.

All told, as reported by *New Brunswick Magazine*, "everybody went to see the show, which was a great one for those times."

As the traveling spectacle made its rounds, the *Royal Tar* did the same. The ship was one of many bearing that moniker in the 1830s—named for William IV, king of the United Kingdom of Great Britain and Ireland from 1830 to 1837. His service in the Royal Navy earned him the highest rank of rear admiral had garnered him the nickname "Sailor King." Many boats throughout England and its provinces were named the *Royal Tar* in allegiance to both King William and the mother country.

Built in 1835 by the Olive Shipyard on the banks of the Saint John River in New Brunswick, the 156-foot-long, two-masted vessel was equipped with two side-mounted paddle wheels, as well as sails. The ship made her trial run on May 2, 1836—a maiden voyage that was chronicled in an article in *New Brunswick Magazine*. The atmosphere aboard the vessel was described as "general jollification," and a hot luncheon was served with "rivers of sherry and oceans of champagne," according to the periodical.

By June 5, the *Royal Tar* had made her first run to St. Andrews, New Brunswick, and then on to Eastport, Maine, on the U.S.-Canadian border. That return trip was completed in a record five hours. The steamer then began making weekly runs as far south as Boston every Wednesday. According to an advertisement in the *New Brunswick Courier*, she left promptly at 7 p.m., and her cost for deck passengers was $1 to Eastport, $3 to Portland, and $5 to Boston.

She was captained by Thomas Reed, who was familiar with the route from St. John Harbour to Portland—the very one she would attempt on her last tragic voyage.

Loaded up with the circus's diverse menagerie, the *Royal Tar* sailed out on Friday, October 21, 1836, carrying twenty-one crew members, seventy-two human passengers, and many more travelers of the non-human variety—including Mogul the elephant, two lions, a Royal Bengal tiger, a gnu (or wildebeest), two pelicans, two camels, several horses, snakes, and an assortment of other birds and reptiles. Also on board was the circus's brass band, a large collection of wax works, and a giant two-ton show wagon (or omnibus).

To make room for all of this, two lifeboats were off-loaded—which would ultimately prove a fatal mistake. Similarly, ever-superstitious sailors believed that carrying birds, snakes, and a brass band on a voyage would herald bad tidings, as would departing on a Friday (long held as an unlucky day to begin a sail). But neither Reed nor his crew subscribed to any of these notions—or if they did, they kept their fears silent.

Spirits were high on the evening the *Royal Tar* set out: The band played for hours and passengers sang and clapped along. Animal tamers also enthralled onlookers by exercising the circus animals on deck. The weather was described as "fine in every respect."

Just as the sun set, however, a high westerly wind blew in. That force continued working against the vessel for several days, eventually forcing Reed to seek shelter for a time in Eastport Harbor (across the bay from New Brunswick, and as far "Downeast" as one can get in Maine).

When Reed finally deemed that it was calm enough to set sail once more, heavy winds moored her again, this time behind Fox Island, not far from Vinalhaven.

As she tarried at anchor, the captain ordered that her boilers be filled. When crewmen set to this duty, they found that the mechanisms were almost dry. They alerted one of the engineers, who told them that they were mistaken. But a few minutes later, the empty boiler became red hot in dangerous proximity to the supports of the adjacent elephant stall. A fire sparked, raged, and spread rapidly, the flames roaring out of human control.

Reed immediately ordered his men to slip anchor, hoist a distress signal, and lower the lifesaving boats. He then climbed into one of these dories with two men, while sixteen other men jumped into the long-board, cut the ropes, and headed for shore.

Meanwhile, the mate and pilot attempted to hoist the sails, enlisting volunteers for help. While they managed to raise the canvas it was quickly devoured by the fire. Sail-less, consumed by a violent, brilliant conflagration, the vessel swung broadside to the waves—or "broached to"—and began drifting down East Penobscot Bay toward the open sea.

Reed watched in horror from the lifeboat, later describing the wreck as a floating "sheet of flame."

Above deck, men, women, children, and animals ran panicked, terrified, choking on the smoke. Due to the intense heat of the fire, clothes were burned off and skin scorched.

Stinson Patten, one of the sixteen crewmen watching helplessly from the lifeboat, later told the *Yarmouth Herald*: "It is impossible to describe the appalling spectacle which the whole scene presented—the boat wrapped in flames, with nearly 100 souls on board, without any hope of relief, rending the air with their shrieks for help; the caravan of wild beasts on deck, ready to tear to pieces all that might escape the flames."

The only hope for survival was to jump overboard; many people did, plunging into the water and immediately sinking, or thrashing around until the numbing waters robbed them of their strength and they drowned.

Others were able to dangle from the side of the enormous funeral pyre on davit tackles, chains, or ropes attached to the rudder. In some cases, the voracious flames ate those ropes away, dropping their human hangers-on into the sea to their deaths.

One passenger, unwilling to part with his monetary possessions, lashed his small trunk to a plank, slid it into the sea where it remained buoyant, then fastened a money belt containing $500 in silver around his waist. He then mounted the taffrail (the rail around the stern) and jumped into the sea. Foresight had not blessed him in his haste, however, and thus leadened by the weight of the silver, he sank fast and drowned.

The accounts of those who survived were full of agony and macabre details.

Circus manager Herbert H. Fuller recalled that he sat on the stern rail until his coat "took fire." He then fastened a rope to the tiller chain and, holding tight, dropped over the stern, where he found "about fifteen others hanging in different places, mostly in the water. In fact, the water washed over all of us almost every minute," he wrote in a letter to a friend that was later published in *The Boston Post*. As he and others clung desperately to their various makeshift life lines, he watched mournfully as several drowned. "Some were beaten from their hold by the waves and some falling into the sea for want of strength to sustain themselves any longer," he wrote. "The screams of women and children; the horrid yells of the men; the roaring of the storm and the awful confusion baffle description."

Having fastened his rope to a chain, which in turn was attached to iron bolts, Fuller's pendulous life preserver held out against the fire and the battering of the sea for much longer than his strength. As minutes became hours and he felt himself flagging, he was able to contort his body so as to twist the rope around his neck and thigh to ease the burden on his aching arms and back. This also allowed him to bear the additional weight of three equally desperate men and a woman who grabbed onto him and "hung securely to me." They remained in this prone position until their rescue, unable to ignore or shut out the ongoing horror around them.

Nearby, Captain Atkins, the pilot, held a woman up with his foot; when her arms failed, he caught her head with his feet and held her full five minutes, "till she washed off, and she drifted by; a kind wave washed her up against an Irishman hanging on my left, and she seized hold of him, and assisted perhaps by our encouraging, and the Irishman's also, kept up."

Another passenger from Portland named Waite was also hanging on for his life while clasping tightly to a small trunk that contained his worldly possessions, including $5,000. However, when he saw a woman struggling against the waves, his humanity got the better of him, and he dropped the trunk into the ocean in order to pull her free. The case sunk and was never recovered.

Meanwhile, a group of men still aboard the *Tar* worked desperately to construct a raft from charred remains of deck boards. But just as they were about to push their makeshift float off the side of the burning vessel, the elephant's huge form loomed above them, "balanced for a terrifying moment at the taffrail" and then smashed down onto on the raft. Its intense weight submerged the float and drowned the men.

Passenger William Marjoram, for his part, recalled seeing a lion in a cage on deck and recited Psalm 57:4, "My soul is among lions. I lie even among those that are set on fire." The devoutly religious man later wrote a piece for the periodical *Zion's Advocate*, describing the scene as nothing less than "truly awful."

As the bedlam and terror played out in its various forms, a U.S. Revenue Cutter, the *Veto*, attempted to approach the fiery wreck. But Captain Howland T. Dyer was worried about getting too close, as the *Veto* was loaded with gunpowder. According to reports, Captain Reed eventually made his way over to the cutter, and took charge. He steered it in as close as safely possible to the *Royal Tar*.

By this point, some survivors had hung precipitously over the icy sea from the sides of the burning ship for nearly two hours.

Reed and Dyer quickly set to rescuing them, aided in their efforts by survivors who still had the strength (or were fueled by the pure adrenaline of their ordeal). Marjoram was among those who helped pull people to safety. One of his most poignant, morose memories involved a woman who had held as long as she could onto the bowsprit with a child in her arms as her clothes completely burned off. When she finally lost her strength, she dropped into the sea. Although she was eventually rescued, her baby drowned.

The *Royal Tar*'s final survivor was taken away shortly before sunset—the nearly catatonic, badly-burned woman had watched both her sister and her daughter perish in the tragedy.

Of the 93 people aboard, 32 passengers and crew members died as the result of burning, drowning, or hypothermia.

Meanwhile, every animal was believed lost. Many assumed that the birds, gifted with flight, had been able to escape—but the remainder of the animals were no luckier than their human shipmates. Some witnesses onshore recalled seeing the horses jumping overboard, then swimming round and round the vessel in a frenzy until they fatigued and sank. Had they swum toward shore, many surmised, they likely could have been saved.

Mogul's hulking corpse was discovered a few days later, floating near Brimstone Island (an unfortunately coincidental name). Still, this didn't stop one far-fetched rumor that the pachyderm had swam up to an island where he "quietly installed himself in a barn."

As for the ship, the *Royal Tar*'s smoldering hulk drifted for several miles before disappearing from sight—and from history. As it carried no insurance, the losses were estimated at $200,000, including receipts from the caravan's tour, the value of the circus creatures, wagons, and other gear, and the many personal possessions of the passengers and crew.

Not long after the disaster, blame was cast about as easily as the tides—from the engineer, to the second engineer, the fireman, Reed, and even Dyer of the *Veto* (who in initial reports was painted as meek, even a coward, due to his initial hesitance to approach the *Royal Tar*).

The Eastern Argus newspaper provided one scathing example, printing that, "we do not hesitate to say that her destruction, so far from being the effects of pure accident, was the result of gross carelessness."

Reed, though, begged to differ, asserting that, "It was pure accident." Shortly after the wreck while still recovering from the ordeal, he wrote that, "I am very stiffened from overexertion, but hope to be better shortly. The people here have been very kind indeed, and we are as well off as can be expected."

Ultimately concluding that "there was no time to think of anything but life," he asked the steamship company to forward survivors free of charge to their destinations.

Several weeks after the catastrophe, Captain Ezekiel Jones of the U.S. Revenue Cutter *Morris* was sent to investigate, interview principals, and lead efforts to recover and bury bodies. Upon visiting the maligned Dyer, he described a man who was "seriously wounded and burnt in several places; and his treatment of the unfortunate since the disaster, has endeared him to every friend of humanity. Many of them have been fed and clothed at his expense, and in doing this he has to my knowledge distressed himself and his family." Yet, Jones added, he was "too much modesty ever to represent his own case; he is universally admitted to be a first-rate public servant, and withal a very gentlemanly man."

Over the ensuing weeks and months, Maine and Canadian newspapers carried letters of thanks from survivors—and, later, some issued corrections about their reports, specifically their characterization of Dyer.

Reed, meanwhile, was universally praised; one passenger passionately credited him for his "deliberate and manly perseverance throughout the whole calamity," which resulted in the saving at least 40 to 50 people. He was officially recognized for his heroism by the federal government, and presented with a $700 reward. He went on to become harbormaster at Saint John, where he was a regular, picturesque figure along the waterfront, often seen accompanied by his dog.

Because it was such a bizarre spectacle, the tragedy of the *Royal Tar* quickly became legendary. Authors and historians penned accounts of its demise, and artists set paint to canvas. One famous rendering depicts the majestic ship—flying the Canadian flag—engulfed in flames, camels and giant cats tumbling off its sides, the choppy waters around it adrift with helpless people, horses, even a tusked elephant, trunk raised aloft.

And in those days, just as now, bad jokes were circulated, including one tasteless rhyme:

> *The* Royal Tar, *she went too far,*
> *Her boiler got too hot;*
> *She'll never see St. John again,*
> *Because she's gone to pot.*

Still, more than 180 years later, her story continues to compel—and, perhaps, the notorious demise of the *Royal Tar* also serves as an apt reminder that the sea, when claiming victims, shows no mercy or discrimination.

8

THE NUBBLE

OMENS AND EMBLEMS

"The sleep of reason produces monsters."
—Francisco Goya (etching)

It was the dull of dawn, an unrecognizable shoreline. A plague of horror hung over it; all was silent. Even the gulls were muted and sobered by the scene.

Drifting in the waves, washing into shore, were wooden boxes. No, not just boxes—coffins.

At least six or seven of them, although it was difficult to be sure as they mixed in so easily with the flotsam and jetsam.

And there was a voice, dank and hollow and dripping with death. It said a name, then prophesized: "You will be among them."

The seasoned sailor jolted awake, eyes like discs, breath fast and jagged.

He drifted in the fuzzy twilight between sleeping and waking, the horrible dream still gripping his mind. No, not a dream, a nightmare. Or an omen?

He was scheduled to leave the next morning on the maiden voyage of the *Isidore*, a ship bound from Kennebunkport Harbor to the port of New Orleans.

Being a man of the sea, he was prone to superstition. He lay awake the rest of that night; the coffins floated at the forefront of his mind as they had in the frozen sea of his dream.

The next morning, still shaken, he told his captain about his nightmare. The old salt laughed off the other man's fear with a hearty pat on his back before angrily ordering the sailor to his station.

The man did as he was told, and set to preparing the ship with the other dozen members of the crew. A few hours later, it set sail—never to be seen again in its terrestrial form.

The *Isidore*—sometimes spelled *Isadore*, derived from ancient Greek and translating to "gift of Isis"—broke to bits on Bald Head Cliff just north of the Nubble in 1842. In the centuries since, the sea tragedy has become legend, rife with superstition and dread, death and unsettled spirits.

Her horrendous wreck prompted officials to investigate erecting a lighthouse on the Nubble, a rocky outcropping just a few hundred feet offshore of Cape Neddick in York—although it would take another 35 years before the sentinel, one of Maine's most iconic, was erected.

Under the direction of thirty-six-year-old Captain Leander Foss, the 396-ton *Isidore* pulled up anchor on November 30, 1842, carrying a crew of fifteen, headed for New Orleans with a cargo of lumber, hay, and potatoes.

From the very beginning—that is, as early as the first nails began banging its structure into place—the vessel seemed shrouded in a cloak of doom. While it is only natural for work crews to engage in banter and singing and storytelling to help pass the time, the *Isidore*'s work site was mostly maudlin, gloomy and silent, save for the sounds of hammering and sawing.

Omens appeared as the day of its launch drew closer and closer. There was the sailor who dreamt of the coffins and similar nightmares of would-be crewman Thomas King.

Several nights before the vessel's departure, King literally jumped out of bed upon waking from a terrible dream. In it, he saw a wrecked ship surrounded by bloated corpses. As the lifeless bodies floated in the salty brine, their faces stiffened into stone. Fog came in, not on cat's feet but on lion's paws, snatching away everything except the ship's skeletal hull.

It shocked him awake—startling his sleeping wife, too—but troubling as it was, it dissipated, as dreams often do, as he went about his daily business.

But the next night, he had the exact same dream. And then once more. Each night these ghastly narratives added more terrifying details.

In one iteration, King found himself standing alone. Confused, he looked back and saw eighteen empty coffins. He asked what they were for, and his captain replied that there was one apiece for each of his crew but "I was so poor there was none for me," King later recalled.

In another version, King volunteered to save the sail and began climbing up into the rigging. As he got as high as the yardarm—the spar on a mast where sails are set—he spotted a large flat rock and leapt onto it. Except it was not a rock—it was his wife and child, who he jumped over while in the throes of his night terrors. Jolted into consciousness, he found himself standing in the middle of the floor.

These nightly convulsions ultimately cemented the young sailor's resolve. "It made an impression that something would happen to the vessel and no threats or persuasion could induce me to go to sea in her," he said later.

But when he told Captain Foss of the dream, the captain not only laughed it off, but scolded him. Foss was known to be dependable and experienced, not prone to superstition. He had a duty to fulfill, and he expected his crew to do the same. Plus, he had paid every crewmember in advance as a means to ensure they would not worry for their families while they were out at sea for a month. King begged to be let out of his contract, or at the very least, that the voyage be delayed.

Yet Foss refused to budge, and the ship's departure remained on schedule.

November 30 was dreary and overcast, the air so cold it could crack bones. As the *Isidore* prepared for launch, the crowd watching from the Kennebunkport docks was decidedly subdued. Normally, they would be clamorous and rowdy, but this group didn't put much oomph into their cheering and waving as they saw their friends and family members off. It seemed much more like an ending than a beginning, as some would later say.

The mood was further dampened when the ship rocked and lilted as it was lowered down its ramp into the sea. However, once it was christened into the waters, it righted itself to the relief of onlookers.

But as the morning grew into afternoon, the temperature grew even bitterer and snow whipped through the air. As Foss took inventory of his ship and crew, he discovered one was missing: Thomas King and his ridiculous portents. He had fled his duties, too terrified to board the forsaken ship. As the bark set off from the harbor, he had hidden in the woods and remained there until he was sure that it was far out to sea.

The captain and his mates cursed him, but the vessel moved out of the harbor nevertheless under the cloak of snow. Soon, she was lost to view, and the crowd dispersed.

The *Isidore* was last seen passing the lonely, rock-strewn outpost of Boon Island. As the night slowly seized its dominion, the winds and waves and snow became ever more overpowering.

And then, the next morning, came the fateful news: The ship had cracked to bits just off Cape Neddick. Its hull was in pieces, lumber floated everywhere, and several bodies washed ashore—seven sailors, including the one whose dream had foretold the disaster.

Captain Foss's body was never recovered, although a stone in Kennebunkport's Village Cemetery bears his name and the inscription:

> *May this event God sanctify,*
> *And thus prepareus (sic) all to die.*
> *That when we leave this earthly clod,*
> *We may be blessed and dwell with God.*

The rest of the retrieved bodies are reportedly buried in common, unmarked graves.

As for those who were never found? Some believe they were cursed to sail the seas for eternity, a bath toy to Poseidon's whims.

Not long after the wreck, reports began circulating about a mysterious ship resembling the *Isidore*. Mariners who claimed to have seen it described a phantom ship manned by a crew of gaunt men dressed in tattered rags, their faces blank, eyes empty.

Whatever the reader believes, though, the legend of the *Isidore* lives on.

A Maine Icon

Had the Nubble Lighthouse been in place in 1824—as locals had lobbied for, for decades—the tragedy may have been thwarted.

Or perhaps the sailors, facing the same brutal weather, would have wrecked elsewhere, sailing off into another legend.

But as history has taught us, the breadcrumb trails of "what-ifs" are fruitless and endless ones.

Before being bestowed with its current name—"nubble" meaning "small knob" or "lump"—the roughly 2-and-a-half acre island was known as Savage Rock. The name came from English explorer Captain Bartholomew Gosnold, who held a parlay with Indians there in 1602.

The ship's historian, John Brereton, recounted that the natives were naked, save for deer skins about their shoulders and seal skins around their waists. Being "swart" in color, they were "strong and well-proportioned," with hair tied in knots and paint adorning their bodies.

"They spoke diverse Christian words," he recalled, "and seemed to understand much more than we, for want of language to comprehend."

A largely barren, jagged hump that juts forth out of the Atlantic, the island has long been distinguished for its characteristic rock formations, which have been chiseled away over millennia. From the air, its craggy outcroppings appear to hold the sea in a tight, imposing grip.

Among those is the legendary Devil's Oven, a dangerous precipice with a 50-foot drop, and Washington's Rock, where visitors and locals have claimed to see the face of the nation's first president.

All of this has also spelled death for countless sailors and ships.

Finally, following many tragedies, a lighthouse was put into service in July 1879. Quintessential and literally postcard-worthy, it consisted of a 40-foot white brick tower standing 92 feet above the sea, accompanied by a quaint red-roofed keeper's house (and two other pitched-roof outbuildings).

Thirty-two cast iron spiral steps and a ship's ladder led to the lantern room, which overlooked the craggy, wave-tossed outline of York Harbor. (Because of its perilous rocks, many keepers were said to have tied their children to posts, or the lighthouse ladder, to ensure they didn't wander off and hurt themselves.)

Still, it is one of the few stations in the state that many lighthouse keepers have been reluctant to leave, and the town of York has wholeheartedly embraced it as its own.

Today, the lighthouse is one of the most photographed in Maine; hundreds of thousands of people visit its home at Sohier Park every year.

The Nubble is so emblematic, in fact, that its digitized image was included in the *Voyager II* space probe's "Golden Record," which was sent out in 1977 to explore the outer planets of our solar system (and potentially discover alien life). The spacecraft's Record, among other things, was etched with 115 images, including those of the Taj Mahal and the Great Wall of China. The Nubble was chosen to represent the seashore, and, thus, humankind's preferred proximity to water, according to Jon Lomberg, the Record's design director. The waves could help extraterrestrials deduce details about our planet's gravity, atmospheric composition, and surface pressure, he added.

"But the handsome, rugged shore of Maine is a fitting snapshot of the beauty of our planet, whatever else it says," he told Smithsonian.com.

It says much more, indeed.

Beauty and death—how often they intertwine.

9

THE DOWNEAST ENIGMA

"Some places speak distinctly. Certain dark gardens
cry aloud for a murder; certain old houses demand to
be haunted; certain coasts are set apart for shipwreck."
—Robert Louis Stevenson

The morning of August 7, 1881 was a rough one. Rough, but not
unmanageable.

Or, so it seemed.

At 8 a.m., two sailors set out in a yawl from their schooner *Vicksburgh*, which was anchored at Seal Harbor on the southeast side of
Mount Desert. Despite there being a strong breeze, a heavy sea, dense
fog, and regular squalls, the two men were confident in their skills and
the small boat's seaworthiness.

Within an hour, though, they were in great peril: The weather and the
sea quickly got the better of their vessel, capsizing it and dumping the
seamen into the turbulent waters.

For three hours they fought for their lives—clinging to the ship's keel,
repeatedly being ripped away by the ceaseless waves, then frantically
regaining their hold. The thick fog and roaring waves prevented anyone
onshore from seeing or hearing them; they were all but helpless as the

prevailing currents succeeded in dragging them farther and farther out to sea.

Then, suddenly, the fog lifted, and Isaac H. Grant, keeper of White-head Lighthouse, spotted their boat being tossed and turned in the tide. They were about a mile eastward of the lighthouse.

The light-tender acted quickly, dispatching his daughter to the nearby lifesaving station before launching his boat into the stormy sea. Due to the tempestuous conditions, he threw his sail and ballast (stabilizing structure) overboard to keep from swamping; then he crossed a danger-ous shoal to affect the rescue. Grant and his son Frank yanked the men into their boat, finding them dangerously exhausted and benumbed. What's more, the legs of their trousers had been frayed away as they had fought to grip their boat, and their skin was covered with abrasions and "excoriated for spaces each as large as a man's hand, forming ghastly wounds," according to the rescue account by the United States Life-Saving Service.

Grant and his son did what they could to ease the men—whose names they learned were Thomas Wilson and John Lynch of the Bangor-based schooner *Vicksburgh*—until a larger boat arrived and transferred them to the light station, where they were tended, bandaged, and given food, water, and shelter.

For his part, Grant was awarded a silver medal from the Life-Saving Service for being a "hero of a remarkably prompt and gallant rescue." A career lightkeeper and husband to the fabled heroine Abbie Burgess Grant, he was indicative of the hardy Downeaster who lives by the sea and according to its might and whims.

As we have mentioned, the Downeast area is infamous for its unique hazards—not the least of which is its capricious weather and stealthy rock and shoal formations. These conditions have all set the scene for many shipwrecks, generated countless legends, myths and ghost stories, and made heroes of ordinary citizens and the keepers of the area's many lighthouses.

The Lure of "Wreck Island"

It stands solidarity on a dash of rocks that thrust up out of the ocean. An army of trees grow clustered at a distance—almost as if, over time, they have cowered away from it. Silent and dark, discolored and worn from the incessant gnawing of the elements, the forty-five-foot-tall brick tower retains a watchful, yet mournful air.

Franklin Island Light was built on its twelve-acre namesake island in 1807. It is Maine's third-oldest lighthouse, but its light has long since been shuttered and its outbuildings were purposely burnt down by the federal government. Uninhabited by humans, Franklin Island is located just six miles off the coast of Friendship, a picturesque town with a quaintly welcoming name, and is central to St. George's River bay.

The area has the distinction of being a key maritime hub, yet it is also considered one of the most dangerous locations on the Maine coast. That is largely "owing to the great number of dry and sunken ledges that swarm in every direction," according to a report penned in 1842 by the Lighthouse Board.

Not surprisingly, then, the island has been a silent witness to many sinkings and drownings—so many in fact that it has earned the nicknames "False Franklin" and "Wreck Island." The latter rather cryptic moniker also underscored the need for a lighthouse on its shores.

One such wreck dates to December 1768, nearly forty years before the lighthouse was installed.

The *Winnibec*, sailing from Boston, lost her bearing in a winter storm. She crashed to pieces on Franklin's dangerous ledges, and her eleven passengers and crew members either drowned or succumbed to hypothermia.

Later, after the storm cleared, a group of fishermen from the mainland followed a waterlogged trail of debris to what ended up being the ship's final port.

Being the first to discover the tragedy, they were overcome by greed, taking the opportunity to loot the destroyed ship and disturb the stiffened, frozen bodies that were scattered along the shore. (In some versions of the story, they were even said to have murdered those survivors who barely clung to this world.)

Making several trips, they transported several kegs of alcohol, barrels of food, firearms, jewelry, and clothing back to their home port.

But their avarice (and the cruel goddess of irony) got the best of them: during their final trip back with their score, a fateful gale blew in and stranded them on Franklin. Using materials from the *Winnibec* to create a makeshift shelter, they hunkered down for the night, still reveling in the luck of their chance find.

Not for long, however.

In the middle of the night, after gorging themselves on food and drink meant for the dead ship and her crew, they were awoken by intruders that they at first mistook for a rescue party. That was, until they got a better look. These visitors had gaunt, hollow eyes; their pallor was a deathly blue; their clothes bloodied and shredded. Ice and crustaceans had formed on their exposed skin, which was cold as the depths of Hades.

Whether it was a mass hallucination, a trick of light and shadow, a prank, or frozen ghost corpses returning to seek revenge, the terrified mariners managed to escape. But they could never shake that haunting memory.

Today, Franklin's loose, craggy oval of land is a national wildlife refuge and bird sanctuary. The area remains beautiful and mysterious. Deemed unnecessary, Franklin Light was purposefully burnt down by the Coast Guard after it was de-staffed in the 1930s. The ruins of the former light-keeping station are now covered in moss and the brick pillars have been torn apart. The tower is all that remains relatively intact, standing tightly bolted-up and surrounded by the architectural ruins of its outbuildings. One can only wonder about the memories and secrets locked up in the tall brick structure as it keeps its lonely perch on the rocks, endlessly looking over the bay.

Just a few miles on a diagonal track to the southeast sits Monhegan Island, whose brine-smeared lighthouse was built in 1824 as a means to prevent shipwrecks in an insidious area that over the years has been identified on charts as "Washerwoman Ledge," "Pulpit Rock," or even "Dead Man's Cove."

The isle also bears a rich—and at times bloody—history.

For starters, there is evidence to suggest that this part of the Downeast played a key role in ancient times: Manana Island, not far from Monhegan, features unique runic scripts that have been dated to the year 1,000, and that some have linked to the Phoenicians or the Vikings (specifically, relatives of the iconic Norseman Eric the Red). Meanwhile, one particularly colorful early story dates to Easter in the year A.D. 575, when an Irish monk named Brendan and a group of his followers landed on Monhegan in a reed boat. They soon discovered wild sheep, selecting one for their holiday meal, then located a safe dry ledge for roasting. But to their surprise, once they had a good fire going, the giant rock began to move—and they realized that it was not a ledge at all, but a giant beast of the deep, most likely a whale (which for reasons only known to them they named "Jasconius").

The outcropping was long used by the natives as a fishing station—"Monhegan" means "the island" in the native tongue—and European explorers relied on it as an important landfall because it was the closest bit of dry land navigationally to Europe in the northeast, and can be seen (in clear weather, at least) for dozens of miles out. As is the case with many colonial settlements, there are numerous early stories of raids by natives on the white man—the latter being either completely wiped out or forced to flee.

Many pirate stories also originate from this locale—including that of the legendary Edward Teach, more commonly called "Blackbeard," Captain Kidd, and his mistress Anne Bonney. Legends of pirates and their treasure are sprinkled like salt throughout the history of seventeenth- and eighteenth-century New England. Raiders and scoundrels alike have been said to roam the waters around the hundreds of islands off the Maine coast, stealing, pillaging, and stashing their goods where they could (ultimately prompting sleuths of all kinds to investigate their "lost" fortunes). Nearly every one of Maine's islands is believed to house some pirate's treasure.

All of this establishes a fittingly dark backdrop for "The Watcher."

Claimed to be seen by many an old timer, this female apparition is believed to be the young wife of a pirate who was left behind to guard hidden treasure. When her husband returned, they were to be wed. But he never came back.

So, it's said, her mournful soul continues to roam the sands, forever on the lookout, forlorn but unwilling to give up hope. Fair-haired, dressed in a flowing dark cloak that never rustles, leaving not a footprint in the sand or crease on the sea grass, she purportedly says over and over: "He WILL come again."

It is a story as enigmatic—and mysterious—as the Atlantic itself.

As Treacherous By Land as By Sea

But perhaps one of the most legendary of Downeast's many isles is Matinicus Rock. Rising out of the ocean like a giant primeval beast, this island is remote, largely treeless, and often gripped by a jealous fog that seems to keep it all to itself.

A thirty-two-acre sliver of granite located roughly twenty-five miles offshore from Rockland, Matinicus was chosen as a prime location for not one, but two, lighthouses in 1827. Constructed of wood (a decision that would quickly be regretted and later rectified) the twin sentinels were positioned forty feet apart and connected by a stone building.

The isolated, wind-whipped island quickly became notorious among lightkeepers, much like the storms that raged around it. They say that during such storms the sea flings the boulders around like pebbles.

The simple act of getting back and forth from Matinicus during calm weather proved treacherous; since it had a little cove but no harbor, boats made their landing by steering as quickly and as steadily as possible through the breakers while, at the other end, being hauled by helpful hands so as to not be dragged back out by the sea.

Keepers didn't last long at this post, perhaps due to the rigors of life on the rock, the lack of readily available medical care, or simply

Matinicus's isolation. Many succumbed to illness or fell victim to tragedy. The lighthouse went through nearly a half-dozen tenders in its first decade.

Gustav Kebbe wrote of the isle's inherent desolation in *The Century Magazine* in 1897; in particular, he relayed a quirky anecdote about a resident cow named Daisy. Mooing "pathetically," she could often be seen "standing on that mass of barren rock, the only living thing in view, the wind furrowing up her hide," he wrote. "She would gaze out at the waste of wild waters with a driven, lonely look, the pathos of which was almost human."

As a somber footnote, he added that the bovine had at one time found companionship in a rabbit, "with which she was accustomed to play at dusk; but the rabbit died."

The rock had a similarly fatal effect on seamen.

One early story involves a British vessel that wrecked just before the close of the American Revolution on what are known as the "northern triangles" between Mussel Ridges and Green Island.

After abandoning ship, the crew rowed away in an open boat toward Castine, but became lost "in the vapor," requiring the men to eventually land at Matinicus. During the ordeal, three of them froze to death; the others arrived onshore in grave condition.

Their British uniforms having been tattered by the sea, the frozen sailors were readily welcomed by locals, who offered them due care and attention.

But so the story goes, as a woman named Aunt Susan was dressing one of the soldiers' frozen hands, she noticed tears in the young man's eyes. When prompted, he mournfully admitted to being one of a party of raiders who had shot and killed her heifer several months prior. Being as it was nearly the end of the war, and the men being so pitiful in their condition, she forgave the transgression.

Curious locals eventually rowed out to the site of the downed ship and spotted one of its cannons, which had broken through the bottom of the rotting boat. Similarly, locals claim that British coins regularly washed up in the area for decades following the wreck.

Another instance from more than a century later illustrates an altogether different brand of valor.

On the decidedly fog-shrouded afternoon of August 19, 1902, "excited cries" suddenly resounded from the ledges off Seal Island (just northeast of Matinicus). These were heard by the so-called King of Seal Island—lone resident W.F. Hill—and his motley crew of guests, who immediately jumped into their dories amidst a bevy of four excitedly barking dogs.

"We knew there was trouble near the ledges," Hill later told the *New York Times*.

Although "it was so thick outside that one could not see five yards ahead," the group was able to make out a three-masted schooner not 100 yards from the island but "fast on the ledges," lilting perilously to her port side, her stern completely awash.

When Hill and his boisterous gang made it aboard, they learned that it was the *Alice M. Davenport*, captained by a Mr. McKown. The bewildered captain could not explain the wreck; all he could say was that the schooner had somehow gotten away from him.

A line was immediately run ashore, and the crew and captain were assisted to dry land. The assorted lot then set to work bringing ashore all the belongings they could.

But suddenly, as Hill recalled, "then came such a deluge of rain as if the heavens had opened its flood gates upon us." At that point, the *Davenport* was pounded and rammed repeatedly against the rocks. The soggy, exhausted party and their rescuers were quickly escorted to Hill's house; he purportedly had twenty-one people "stowed away" at his camp that night.

The following morning, McKown set out for his launch at Vinalhaven—a lobstering village just off the coast—after giving Hill his gun and putting him in charge of the *Davenport*.

Perhaps the captain had inherently sensed danger; not long after his departure a fleet of five or six ships was seen coming up from Long Island, loaded with an "unusual number of men on them," as reported by Hill. They drew up alongside the *Davenport*, and several of their number began clambering up the sides to the deck.

Acting quickly, Hill ordered them to stop. But they ignored him.

Enraged, he drew McKown's revolver. Pointing it toward one of the men, who had his hands on the boat's rails and was just about to bound over it, he threatened: "If you put your foot over that rail, you are a dead man."

This challenge was apparently warning enough. Hill told the *Times* that the men jumped back into their boats, "and finally seeing that I meant business, sailed for home."

Further disaster thwarted—again by a stalwart Downeaster.

A Courageous Soul

But if Matinicus is renowned for anything, it is for its connection to Abbie Burgess (and vice versa).

The unexpected hero moved to Matinicus in 1853 with her respected light-tending father, Samuel Burgess, as well as her invalid mother, three sisters, and brother.

Duties at the original station included constantly tending the whale oil in the lamps so it wouldn't congeal, and cleaning off the thick soot that constantly coated the reflectors. Young Abbie was soon enlisted to assist in that work, in addition to her other responsibilities of keeping house and caring for her mother and younger siblings.

Her tenacious spirit became legend in January 1856. That day, her father departed the island to retrieve supplies from the mainland, leaving seventeen-year-old Abbie in charge.

"I can depend on you Abbie," he told her as he left, expecting to be back later that day or the following morning.

However, a strong gale screamed in, preventing his return.

And not just for a day or two—he was forestalled for four weeks.

Abbie wrote of the relentless weather: "The sea is never still and when agitated it roars, shuts out every other sound, even drowning out our voices."

In its endless fury, the storm largely destroyed the keeper's quarters. Resolute in purpose, Abbie sought refuge for herself, her sisters, and her mother in one of the towers, what she called the "only endurable place." She also waded through water so cold that it felt like it was slicing open the skin to rescue all but one of the family's hapless hens.

And for the entire twenty-eight days she persevered in keeping the light constantly burning.

"For some reason, I know not why, I had no misgivings and went on with my work as usual," she wrote. "Though at times greatly exhausted by my labors, not once did the lights fail."

There was a harrowing case of déjà vu, when, the following year, her father was again detained on the mainland due to stormy weather. This time he was gone for three weeks.

Again, the fastidious young woman rose to the challenge, keeping the family safe and the lights blazing. And her father returned just soon enough; when passage was safe once again, he found his cold, weary family with just one egg and a cup of cornmeal among them.

Samuel Burgess was relieved of his post in 1860, but Abbie stayed on to provide guidance to the new keeper. His son, Isaac Grant, came to the island with him. Isaac and Abbie took a liking to each other, and were soon wed.

They became a light-tending couple, taking up a post at Whitehead Light Station in St. George in 1875—where Grant performed his silver-medal-garnering rescue six years later. They had four children (one of whom, Bessie, died as a toddler).

Abbie died in 1892 at age fifty-two. Before her death, she wrote of the love she had for the lights she had so carefully tended for nearly forty years.

"It has always seemed to me that the light was part of myself," she said, describing how she would watch it most of the night, unable to sleep and plagued by the what-ifs should it be snuffed out. "These old lamps on Matinicus Rock . . . I often dream of them. When I dream of them it always seems to me that I have been away a long while, and I am hurrying toward the Rock to light the lamps before sunset . . ."

In 1923, after being rebuilt twice, the north light was permanently darkened as part of a sweeping, cost-saving reform by the government. The tower remained locked until the Coast Guard took control of life-saving duties in the mid-1900s.

Abbie Burgess now rests at Spruce Head Cemetery in Rockland. In 1945, more than fifty years after her death, author and historian Edward Rowe Snow placed a miniature lighthouse on her grave in honor of her relentless resolve.

The heroine also lives on in numerous books (fiction and nonfiction), songs, historical reenactments, and the U.S. Coast Guard even named a 175-foot buoy tender—located off the coast of Rockland—in her honor.

Abbie had always been concerned with Matinicus's immortality.

"I wonder if the care of the lighthouse will follow my soul after it has left this worn-out body!" she remarked shortly before her death.

Some say that is indeed the case, as woman and isle have immortalized one another in many ways.

Treasure among the Wreckage

The thunderous crack of a hull slicing open as it abruptly met rocks and dry land was the sound that crossed roughly a half-mile of water and coastline to Hendricks Head keeper Jaruel Marr and his wife, Catherine, in the early spring of 1870. This was followed by the vibration of a heavy impact, screams, and cries for help.

Batted about by the ocean and wind, a vessel had smashed against a ledge just seaward of the lighthouse, located on the western side of Southport Island on Maine's midcoast.

Fifteen-foot-high waves pinned the boat in place; as it began to break apart, its passengers and crew attempted to save themselves by climbing up its rigging. But in the frigid temperatures, the torrents of pummeling water quickly froze—locking the doomed seamen in place, the rigging becoming a trap rather than a refuge.

Keeper Marr and his wife could only look on, terrified and heartbroken. To launch their own dory in the vicious storm would only mean their deaths, as well.

Frantic, with no other options, they lit a bonfire to let any survivors know that they were there and would come to help as soon as it was safe. But the storm ceaselessly pummeled the boat and the spit of land, preventing rescue for hours on end.

Darkness began to enshroud the island and its squat, square lighthouse. All hope seemed lost.

Then, the keeper glimpsed something bouncing in the salty waves. Rigging a safety line around his waist, he waded into the breakers, retrieving what turned out to be a small, bundled package.

Soaked and shivering, he returned to the edge of the bonfire.

As the heat from the flames warmed him, he inspected the carefully-wrapped item in his hands. It consisted of two feather beds tied together but nearly soaked through.

Carefully, precisely, he cut it open. Inside was a box. Opening it, he was stupefied at its contents: a baby girl wrapped in a blanket—terrified, writhing, and screaming.

Marr ran inside, where his wife, just as shocked and perplexed, took the infant, calming and feeding her.

And then the couple noticed something tucked inside the blankets wrapped around the baby: a locket, accompanied by a message from her mother that commended her kin to God.

Back outside, the storm raged on. Overnight, the ship was smashed into oblivion. When daylight finally reached its welcoming fingers over the horizon, Marr, his wife, and authorities discovered that there were no survivors; all, except the child, had been consumed by the sea.

This story is one of the most epic in Maine's lighthouse history. Over the years it has inspired numerous children's books and novels, including Toni Buzzeo's *The Sea Chest*, and *Waterbaby* by Chris Mazza.

Although some doubt its validity, calling it too reminiscent of the Biblical story of Moses, descendants of the Marrs'—many of whom went on to become lighthouse keepers themselves—firmly attest its truth.

The baby was believed to be adopted by a doctor and his wife who spent their summers in Southport, and she was said to have quite the fitting name: Seaborne.

Sitting on a unique curvature of land on the cusp of Boothbay Harbor, the circa-1829 Hendricks Head Lighthouse looks out onto a bay of unknowns—the aforementioned wreck being one of the most fabled and mysterious.

A Lifesaving Luminary

Lightning ripped through the pitch-black sky, threatening to tear it apart. The wind clawed and pulled in all directions. The sea was no less vicious, tossing up wave after giant wave and wrenching the small boat about like a piece of cardboard. Its lone passenger was sprayed with water so frigid it felt as if he was being frozen from the inside-out.

As he struggled to keep his craft afloat, the fisherman thought his days were at an end—he had tempted fate so many times out on those dangerous waters, but now the sea was finally going to swallow him up.

Another lightning bolt seared through the immeasurable dark.

And in that brief flicker, he saw a sight that chilled him as much as the tumult of the wind and sea: a reef that was far too close—and standing on it, a woman in a blaze of white, waving her arms in a warding-off gesture. Remarkably, she did not seem to feel the effects of the weather. Rather, she appeared to be insulated from it; her white dress and fair hair were perfectly undisturbed, as if she were merely walking in the park on a bright sunny day. It was only her arms that moved, frantically pantomiming for him to get away.

The fisherman steered his boat in the other direction with all his effort—narrowly avoiding crashing into the ledge at Ram Island. A seasoned sailor of Boothbay, he knew of its notoriously jagged rocks and onerous penchant for sending men to Davy Jones' locker, but blinded by the storm, he had had no idea he had been so perilously close.

The mysterious woman had saved him.

She is known as the "lady in white." No one knows her origin, or who she was—but she appears on Ram Island in the worst weather to warn mariners away from the craggy spit of land. She is part of a long tradition—earthly and otherwise—of sentinels guarding the seas around this island.

Today, a thirty-five-foot lighthouse tower stands just offshore of Ram's ledges. A substantial stone structure of granite and brick, it juts out of the sea, and is connected to the island via footbridge.

It took decades of petitioning by locals to erect the light, the delay due largely to the fact that it was located within a few miles radius of more than a half-dozen other lights in the Boothbay area. Built in 1883, its first keeper was Samuel John Cavanor, an old salt with a peg leg who would have made Captain Ahab proud.

But even with the lighthouse in place, Cavanor continued to report regularly on wrecks, and the tower itself was not immune. Over its 130-year history, its walkway has been destroyed, rebuilt, removed, and rebuilt again, and the lighthouse lantern glass has been smashed and its fog whistle toppled. When the light was automated in the 1960s, it was subjected to both neglect and vandalism, and its antique Fresnel light was even stolen once (although it was later recovered).

The location of many shipwrecks and drownings since the days when men first took to boats, its name "Ram" seems fitting—but it was actually derived from the age-old farming practice of quarantining male sheep away from the mainland as a means to control breeding. Although early settlers are known for their ruggedness and ingenuity, they were not necessarily renowned for their creativity in naming: There are more than a dozen Ram Islands dotting the Maine shore.

Situated at the eastern end of Boothbay Harbor near the mouth of the Damariscotta River, the island is particularly perilous due to its low elevation and the snarling hungry rocks lurking just off its shoreline.

Locals and seafarers had long decried that it could easily be obscured in any kind of weather, from high seas to fog to rain and snow (in truth, anything but calm seas). It was so notorious that it earned the ominous nickname of the "dark old hole."

As a means to thwart disaster, locals at first took the matter of a lighthouse into their own hands. It started out simply enough: In the mid-1800s, when a fisherman nearly shattered his boat on the night-obscured island, he made it his duty to travel out at dusk to tie a lantern down for his fellow mariners to see by.

Others soon came to share the charge, with the unspoken understanding that the first one in from the fishing grounds before sunset was to serve as the de facto lightkeeper.

Sometimes they left a lantern suspended in an anchored dory, or affixed at a high point on the island. One lobsterman even created his own makeshift lighthouse, enclosing a lantern in a box with windows on all four sides and weighted down with rocks.

Over time, however, the practice became spotty, then stopped altogether. It was then, as author and lighthouse keeper Robert Thayer Sterling described, that "the spirit world seemed to have taken a hand."

On a night of "stygian darkness"—that is, as dark as the River Styx of Greek mythology that separates the living world from the dead one—a sailor attempting to make it home to Boothbay reported suddenly seeing a woman standing on the shores of Ram Island, dressed all in white, waving a torch. She seemingly came out of nowhere, warding him away from the rocks just in time.

In another instance, a mariner was convinced he saw a ship consumed in flames on the edge of the island. He had become disoriented in a thick fog and was bound for a collision with the shore just as he spotted it. Later, he returned to the island, but could find no evidence of a wrecked boat nor a fire.

"Not even a might of charred wood could be picked up," Thayer wrote, "and he was at a loss to know how the signal was issued."

Others have seen the lady in white standing stoically on the boat as it is imbued in flames.

In a few stories, she has manifested in sound; one seafaring resident unluckily caught up in two different storms recalled being alerted the first time by a loud ethereal pounding, and the second by the deep tone of a fog signal. In both cases, the dark was impenetrable, but he was able to turn from the sounds just as he barely made out the rocky outline of shore with squinted eyes.

He later learned that there was no fog signal on the island—one would not be installed until 1897.

"He was positive that it came from the spirit world as a warning that he was approaching a dangerous reef," Thayer professed.

Still, no one knows the identity of the willowy woman or her origins. Was she the victim of a shipwreck bound by duty to warn others away from her fate? The widow of a sailor yearning to spare others her heartbreak? Or simply a good Samaritan ghost?

Today, with the lighthouse standing as a beacon at Ram Island, the occasion of her appearance is rare—but her legend lives on.

Emblematic Watcher

As you climb the thirty steps of the narrow spiral staircase with its endless filigrees, the light is muted, the endless tumult of the surf muffled. Then it's a hoist up seven rungs of a wooden ladder, a shimmy through a snug hole in the floor, and you're standing in a claustrophobic lantern room with barely enough space to outstretch one arm.

Surrounding you is a 360-degree view of land and sea. Forever seems visible on the horizon; the ocean stretches on and on, eventually blending with the clouds. Bumps of land in the distance are its only companions. Down below, waves run salty fingers over hundreds of feet of contoured rock, striated and stretched as if the sea has endlessly tugged on it in an attempt to claim it as its own. Caressed smooth by the sea, these unique formations are variegated with contrasting dark and light streaks. Kelp lays abandoned, tide pools offer hidden treasures, and seagulls hunker with a watchful eye for any errant bit of food.

Beside you, the Fresnel lens is a work of art, its ripples of glass creating optical illusions out of the sea and sky.

Up here in the confined, isolated lantern room, it's hard not to be absorbed by the loneliness that comes with the adamant wash of the waves and the whistling of the wind demanding to be let in through the windows. One could forget the whole world exists out here.

Pemaquid Point Lighthouse has kept vigil on this stony outcropping in Bristol for nearly 200 years.

Prior to its raising, the area was the site of many conflicts, including an attack by Dixie Bull the pirate on the prosperous Pemaquid settlement in 1632 ("Pemaquid" is believed to be a native word for "situated far out"); a siege of the English settlement Fort Charles by the French in 1696; and numerous raids—scattered throughout the tumultuous history of the area's colonization—by Abenaki Indians, including during King Philip's War in the 1670s.

Commissioned by John Quincy Adams and put into service in 1827, Pemaquid Point is the quintessential image of a New England lighthouse, with its white, conical brick tower attached to a white cape house. The lighthouse was originally thirty feet tall. It was soon raised to its current height of thirty-eight feet, in order to keep pace with the area's burgeoning maritime and shipping trade—which, not surprisingly, led to an increase in shipwrecks.

Notably, two wrecks from the same day in 1903 have left enduring historical imprints.

On September 17, the fishing boat *George F. Edmunds*, captained by William Poole of Gloucester, and the small coasting schooner *Sadie and Lillie* were lost among the rocks off Pemaquid during the roar and bluster of a vigorous storm. Between the two wrecks, fifteen mariners died and only four were saved. "Nothing but splintered wood and twisted iron remained of the two vessels," the newsletter "The Lincoln County News" reported.

As a tragic denouement, Pemaquid Point resident William P. Sawyer, who interviewed the survivors and penned the event's history of record, was found dead near the lighthouse on September 17, 1945, on the 42nd anniversary of the catastrophe.

Unfortunately, as we have read, tragedy often begets further tragedy.

10

NEPTUNE'S BRIDE

SCORNED BY THE SEA

"Gradually the almost infinite size of this water forced itself on his attention ... Here, faced by the brute obtuseness of the ocean, the miles of division, one was clamped down, one was helpless, one was condemned. . ."

—William Golding

When he came to, it was dawn.

He shifted slightly but felt constrained; he was lashed to something, an object that was noticeably lilting back and forth, constantly bobbing and in motion. He heard the familiar and ever-ceaseless pounding of surf, and the unmistakable creak and groan of damp, bloated wood rubbing against itself. Finally, he blinked open his ice-crusted eyes and saw that he was surrounded by the ocean.

He was in a precarious position, alright—a few hours before, he had tied himself to the mast of a slowly sinking ship. He could see the ledge it had hit just cresting out of the water below, and could just make out the hazy outlines of land nearby.

Those things, but nothing else.

The benumbed, weary man struggled to remember the night's events; in his mind, which had become prone to hallucination due to exposure, it all seemed to draw out into eternity.

He was sure of one thing, though: He was alone, and completely prone to the sea.

In late September 1860, *Neptune's Bride* had had a seemingly successful fishing excursion: On the 22nd, the 90-ton fishing schooner was returning to its home port in Gloucester, Massachusetts, from a cruise in the Gulf of Maine that had yielded 105 barrels of mackerel.

But that evening, as it was crossing through Penobscot Bay, the weather turned tempestuous—some reports called it a "gale," others merely a "storm." In any case, the schooner was "jogging along under foresail" around 10 p.m. when suddenly it rammed the rocks of Malcolm Ledge, an outcropping that lies midway between Wooden Ball Island and Seal Island (and is a long eighteen miles from the Maine coast).

Save for the night watch, the thirteen crew members had gone below deck for the night. They were jolted awake upon impact, and they rushed on deck and made for the single dory amidst blinding fog, rain, and wind that threatened to rip the rescue boat right out of their grip.

The men managed to get the dory over the side, and eleven of their number—including ship's master Jacob Olsen of Gloucester—jumped in. Two of the crew, Joseph Marsh and Henry Johnson, opted to stay aboard the sinking ship, thinking it the better of two losing options. Also, they feared their added weight would further endanger the overloaded dory.

Sadly for their shipmates, their calculation proved correct: Heavy seas swamped the would-be life craft nearly as soon as it launched, and its water-logged occupants took refuge back on the exposed ledge. Bereft of its human cargo, their dory was quickly swept away in the waves.

Facing a heavy sea and a rapidly-rising tide—the unfortunate "perfect storm" of conditions—the stranded seamen realized that they had to attempt to return to their sinking ship. Still on deck, Marsh and Norwood attempted help, unsuccessfully throwing and rethrowing a line out to their desperate shipmates.

All the while, the storm intensified, and *Neptune's Bride* continued to break apart on the ledge beneath the men's feet. With the waters rising around them and the ship dipping lower and lower, Marsh and Norwood watched helplessly as their shipmates were ripped away, one by one, by the agitated sea. Neptune himself seemed to make quick work of their demise; within minutes, they had all been washed off their disappearing perch and drowned.

And still, the hungry sea continued to climb. To escape its rising depths, Marsh and Norwood grappled up into the doomed vessel's rigging. As the water continued its slow, deliberate ascent, coming closer and closer to the men's perch at the very top of the mast, all seemed hopeless.

Marsh, seemingly over-confident in his swimming skills and thinking it his only means of survival, leapt into the water and headed off for Seal Island, located about a mile away.

But just a few minutes later, Norwood, despite the clamorous, howling winds and waves, heard the man yell, "Oh my God!" and watched as he was swallowed by the waves.

For his part, Norwood kept his loving wife and young child front of mind, refusing to give up hope. He was determined to hang on as long as possible. That hope was hard to hold onto, however, as the tide continued to follow, threatening to fully engulf him in a slow, torturous drowning—first rising to his feet, then creeping up his legs to his knees, then sliding its icy fingers up to his waist.

As if this gradual mental and physical torment wasn't enough, sometime in the oblivion of the endless night, the sky rent open, sending forth coursing rain and piercing lightning bolts. Neptune, it seems, was not only enraged, but had enlisted friends.

Prone, exhausted, and growing ever weaker, Norwood realized that he was losing consciousness—and somehow the seaman found the strength and wherewithal to lash himself to the mast with a length of rope he had salvaged during the wreck.

Then he passed out.

It was in that pitiful position that he awoke a few hours later amidst the rescuing dawn.

And it was where he stayed the rest of that achingly-slow, agonizing day, suffering from thirst, hunger, exposure, and delirium.

After eighteen hours, the tide began to turn and slink toward him once more, and his slipping mind grappled to gain hold of the prospect that he might spend another night crucified, as it were, on the ship's sinking, rotting bones.

Then suddenly, he sensed motion in the water below.

Steadily, it moved closer and closer, until finally his confused mind made sense of the scene, and recognized his salvation: two harried men in a rowboat, calling out to him.

The pair freed Norwood—who by this time, as they recalled later, was more dead than alive—from his perch, loaded him into their boat, and rowed him to their fishing shack on nearby Seal Island. Inside, they prescribed him the prevailing cure-all of the day—a strong drink of whiskey—then put him to bed with hot stones beneath his feet.

This rescue was later described by Vinalhaven historian Sidney Winslow as "the merest accident." At around 5 p.m. on September 23, the two fishermen had spotted the wreck by chance while out mending their nets. Insistent that he saw a man in the topmast, one of the fishermen persuaded the other to row out to investigate.

The following day, with Norwood beginning to mend from his ordeal, the men brought him to Vinalhaven, where he was given medical attention. He was then put up in the town's hotel, where he remained until he was strong enough to make the return trip to his family in Gloucester.

And, despite the intense loss and his doubtless mental and physical anguish, he was pleased to find that he was not the sole survivor, after all.

Henry Johnson was one of the eleven members of the crew who jumped into the dory when *Neptune's Bride* abruptly ran upon the ledge. When the small craft almost immediately swamped, he was able to hold fast and remain inside as his shipmates clung to the eroding safety of Malcolm Ledge.

Although it was practically awash and at the same time both sinking and drifting out to sea, he bailed as hard as he could until exhausting himself. But his effort paid off: He not only reduced the water level in the boat, but had the chance opportunity of spotting and snagging several empty barrels, listless debris from *Neptune's Bride*. These he fastened to the sides of the boat, which kept it afloat while also preventing it from catching in the wind.

Still stranded but his life (at least for the time being) spared, Johnson gave in to his fatigue, curling up in the bottom of the boat and immediately falling asleep. Over the next several hours, his odd, makeshift vessel drifted around Penobscot Bay, safely carrying its unconscious passenger.

The next morning, the storm subsided—and the bone-tired sailor was startled awake with the cry: "Ahoy, on the boat! Stand by to board!"

Sitting up, rubbing at his eyes, Johnson found himself in the protective shade of a schooner: The *Anne*, captained by a man named Henderson and headed for Belfast.

Deliriously overjoyed by his rescue, Johnson clambered into the fishing boat, which carried him on to safety.

Later, he and Norwood were reunited—and ultimately forever bonded by their shared experience aboard the ill-fated *Neptune's Bride*. Of the ship's thirteen-man crew—an ominous number to begin with, for a seaman, landlubber, or otherwise—the two were the only ones who lived to tell the tale of the scorned bride of the sea.

11

CAPE ELIZABETH

HEROISM DEFINED

"A hero. You want to be one of those rare human beings who make history, rather than merely watch it flow around them like water around a rock."

—Dan Simmons

It was the last thing he expected to see as he looked out his cottage window that frigid December morning in 1875—although here, on the southern end of Maine's flinty, rock-ribbed coastline that sent so many vessels to their waterlogged graves, it surely was not out of the ordinary.

A ways off in the distance, standing at the crag of Watt's Point, a man was waving his arms and hat frantically, in an apparent signal of distress.

Alarmed and quick to help, Otis N. Wheeler ran over to the home of his neighbor and friend, John O. Philbrick, and the two immediately set out in the near-zero temperatures to their dory at the shore. Working against strong, biting, and clawing northwesterly winds, the pair rowed across the ledge running along Richmond Island, to a point nearly a quarter-mile offshore.

They were able to land near a small fishing schooner that had been stranded on the rocks. Its hull had been ruptured and she was sharply lilted. Two figures were hunkered on the boulders nearby.

Securing their dory against the lashing winds and tide, and taking cautious steps along a ledge that had been slicked by wind-whipped spray, Wheeler and Philbrick made their way over to the men. One, they found, was just a boy, hunched and stumbling around in an attempt to keep warm. By his feet was the other, lying motionless in a pitted, icy crevice. They first feared him dead until, leaning in close, they could hear him faintly moaning.

Moving back along the sheer ice, Philbrick and Wheeler steadied the upright young man and loaded him safely into their dory, then carefully cradled and carried his shipmate back across the slippery ledge. The return trip was no less hazardous, as the pair worked against contrary seas and strong headwinds—and were swamped and soaked by polar waves over and over again—until they worked clear of the reef and made it safely back to Broad Cove. There, they carried the incapacitated fishermen to Wheeler's cottage, cutting away their boots and clothing and immersing their blistered, bloated, discolored feet and hands in water.

Leaving them to rest in the care of his neighbor, Wheeler then rowed his dory about a mile through tumbling waters to the mainland of Cape Elizabeth, where he asked the local merchant to alert authorities, and purchased rum, liniment, corn meal, coffee, and a few other necessities.

After making the dangerous trek back home, he and Philbrick sat up with the bedridden young men for thirty some-odd hours, nursing their injuries and attending to their needs. As the shipwrecked men started coming to, they began to relate their tale.

The day before their shipwreck on November 30, they had left the eastern end of Casco Bay on a course for Boston. Soon after they departed, gale force winds rampaged in; they kept close to shore to avoid the brunt of them, but then ran right into heavy fog, immediately losing their bearings. Their boat then ran upon Watt's Point around 9 p.m.

As Wheeler had not noticed them until looking out his cottage window at 9 a.m., then that meant they had been exposed to the elements for thirteen hours. During the night, they recalled, they had been forced to stand in water that rose more than a foot deep around them (as normal high tide completely covers the ledge).

Meanwhile, as the men were on the mend and readily telling their tale, the report of their ship's demise had been relayed to Portland, and the Revenue Service cutter *Dallas* made its way to Richmond Island. Its crew set ashore, retrieved the two sailors and carried them back to the city, where each fully recovered. It was later reported that, upon questioning the pair, authorities found great discrepancies in their story and learned that they had, in fact, stolen the boat at Falmouth Foreside, raided a schooner lying in nearby Portland Harbor, then had headed for "parts unknown" before the storm threw a literal dent in their plans.

Nevertheless, in the following June of 1876, Wheeler and Philbrick were presented second-class Medals of Honor for brave and unselfish efforts by the U.S. Life-Saving Service.

Throughout its tenure spanning 1874 to 1914, the Service awarded 900 such medals—nineteen of those to Mainers, both professional lifesavers and ordinary citizens alike. Wheeler and Philbrick were the first-ever to ever receive the awards for their heroism on that brutal morning of December 1, 1875—a testament to their innately hardy and heroic nature.

Courage, Without a Whim

Cape Elizabeth has been the setting for not one, but two, history-making rescues (and undoubtedly many more that were never recorded; perhaps it is the very nature of living by the sea that prompts one to instinctually spring to action in a crisis).

The waters along the beatific city's shores have claimed many victims, both human and vessel. The *Charles* was the first recorded shipwreck involving loss of life. On July 12, 1807, the packet schooner (a vessel built to carry people and higher-value goods, as compared to a more rustic fishing schooner) ran into a ledge in thick fog while traveling between Portland and Boston. Of the twenty-two people aboard, only six survived. The victims included Captain Jacob Adams, who at first swam to shore to save his own life, then drowned when returning to save his wife (who had also drowned), and twenty-four-year-old Lydia Carver of Freeport. This young lady's story was particularly mournful, as she was returning from Boston where she had purchased her wedding dress for her upcoming nuptials. Her lifeless body was discovered on the beach next to a trunk containing the sodden gown.

It was more than seventy-five years after this catastrophe, in 1885, that Cape Elizabeth Two Lights keeper Marcus Aurelius Hanna solidified his well-earned stature in Maine maritime history.

Fittingly named for the last of the so-called Five Good Emperors of Rome, the Bristol, Maine native, Civil War veteran, and career light-tender was assigned to the Cape Elizabeth lighthouse in 1873 following a previous post at Pemaquid Point Lighthouse in his hometown.

By that time, the sentinel, most iconically rendered by twentieth-century painter Edward Hopper, had gone through many different iterations. The lighthouse was initially built in 1811 and then, when that structure proved inadequate against the battering of the sea and the rapidly increasing boat traffic in Casco Bay, it was refortified with its second tower seventeen years later (thus earning it the nickname "Two Lights").

Nevertheless, the reinforced light signal couldn't save the schooner *Australia*. The vessel collided with Dyer's Ledge below the light station's fog signal around midnight on January 22, 1885, in the midst of a heavy blizzard, temperatures far below zero.

Built in Southport, Maine, and carrying 150 barrels of mackerel, as well as a cargo of guano and ice (one can only wonder about the nature of that unusual combination), the 62-ton schooner had left Boothbay Harbor bound for Boston late the previous afternoon. Captain John W. Lewis incorrectly anticipated a routine voyage due to light northerly breezes and clear skies. Instead, his ship ran into snow, heavy winds, and near-zero temperatures.

Around midnight, the vessel reached Halfway Rock, midway across Casco Bay. With visibility deteriorating by the minute, Lewis and his crew scanned the horizon for the lighthouse's welcoming beams—one steady, one blinking—while straining to make out its whistle. Finally, they heard the repeated, faint sound of a horn and immediately set their course toward it—but by the time they realized that it was from the Portland-Boston steamer *Tremont*, it was far too late.

They were off-course, disoriented, and the squall continued to increase in its furious intensity. Repeated sprays of ice swamped the deck, freezing fast to everything exposed to the open air, including lines. The ship was becoming unresponsive and giving into Poseidon's whims; the crew were unable to tack. To make matters even grimmer, the wind ripped away their mainsail. In an attempt to gain control of the ship and prevent her from breaking up, Lewis and his men resorted to throwing their valuable loads of fish overboard.

Then, they heard Two Light's distinctive fog signal. His options quickly running out, the captain decided to run the vessel aground as near to the sound of the signal as possible. Having drifted dangerously close to land, there was simply no way they could ever work offshore with the ship in its near-frozen condition.

Just around 8 a.m., the *Australia* struck the cape 200 yards southwest of the fog signal building, coming to a halt about a hundred feet from shore. The men, to avoid being swept overboard, scrambled up into the rigging and entwined their arms and legs with the ice-crusted lines.

And there, they waited.

As the ship lay at a 45-degree angle on her starboard side, caught on the treacherous rock that formed the shoreline, momentous waves broke against her stern, quickly gnawing away her house and galley. She was slowly deteriorating below the men's feet and before their very eyes. Freezing, debilitated, and stranded on the ship's masts, the men kept their eyes on the towers above for any sign of rescue.

Lewis, losing control and sensing death, purportedly began rambling about dying and sobbed, "God help my wife and poor children!" Although he held fast to the ship, desperately trying not to lose his grip as the vessel was dashed to oblivion, the waves inevitably proved too strong. He was knocked from his perch into the water, and struggled briefly until the waters consumed him.

For what must have felt like an eternity, the tower's keeper remained ignorant to this suffering. That was, until around 8 a.m.

Relieved of his overnight duty by the fog signal at 6 a.m., Hanna had retired to the keeper's house. He was recuperating from a nasty virus, having spent the previous few days and nights ill in bed. At that hour, the temperature at the station was -4 degrees.

The light-tender placed his wife temporarily in charge of the lights, and at 7:10 a.m., Mrs. Hanna climbed the ladders to the east and west towers, extinguishing both lanterns and readying them for relighting that evening. This laborious, meticulous process took more than an hour.

Having completed her duties, she was about to descend the west tower when she looked out and saw the indistinct profile of the *Australia* just beyond the fog signal station. She ran to the house and alerted her husband, who, despite his sickness, quickly dressed and ran down to the station, where his assistant Hiram Staples had been keeping watch, completely unaware of the crisis below.

Retrieving his shocked and embarrassed assistant, Hanna worked his way down the ledges, where he could see the crippled vessel and what seemed to be two lifeless forms hanging in its rigging—and then one of them weakly waved and called out to him.

Knowing that it would be impossible to launch a boat in such an angry sea, Hanna retrieved a long length of rope and tied it to a heavy piece of iron—this after bashing open a door of an outbuilding with an axe, rather than waste precious minutes retrieving the key and shoveling away the snow piling its door.

He and Staples then rushed to the edge of the surf once again, where the lightkeeper attempted again and again to throw the weight and its connected line out to the ship. But he was fighting winds that had since whipped themselves into gale-force, and the ocean mockingly sprayed icy water at him—pelting his face, blinding him, freezing and penetrating his clothing and boots. Soon, unable to manipulate his fingers, he crawled behind a rock for relief, beating and stomping at his hands and feet to regain circulation.

As he was doing so, a tremendous wave suddenly lifted the vessel "sheer from the rocks and she came down with a thundering crash," as Hanna recalled later, smashing her portside inward and flipping her over. This left two of her crew, Irving Pierce and Austin Kellar, dangling ever-more precariously just above the waves. As they were flipped unnaturally forward and working against gravity, the men were unable to free themselves from the tangle of the rigging (at first their savoir, now their captor).

Ever more determined, Hanna waded into the surf up to his waist—and after nearly two dozen tries, he was able to land the iron weight on the sloping deck. Pierce grabbed it and bent it around his waist. He had by this time worked himself mostly free of the rigging, as well as his boots and some of his clothing; despite his dangerously frozen condition, he was concerned that the soaking weight of his garments might pull him down and drown him, and he wanted to do all he could to increase his buoyancy.

With a great strength of will, placing complete trust in his rescuers, he plunged into the water. Hanna painstakingly hauled him through the violent waves to shore. As he would write later, he "in some way—I don't know how—got this frozen lump of humanity to a place out of the reach of the surf."

But his duty was only half done. With the wreck continually battered and breaking up, he removed the line from Pierce, waded out into the glacial, numbing waters, and threw repeatedly toward the ship again. Taking fewer tries this time, he landed the weight, and Kellar grabbed it, wound it around himself, and jumped into the surf.

Hanna, now beyond exhausted, was able to yank the man halfway in, then ceded the effort to Staples and a group of neighborhood men who had come running to help, rounded up by Hanna's son.

According to the official Life-Saving Service report, Pierce was in grave condition: "his jaws were set and he appeared to be almost gone." Hanna described him as "totally blind from exposure to the cold," adding that, "the expression on his face I shall not soon forget."

With the intense storm unyielding, and the mounting snowdrifts and harsh cold too intense for an immediate transfer to Hanna's house several hundred yards away, the rescuers opted to carry the two ailing sailors to the fog signal station. There they stripped them of their icy garments, gave them food and liquids, and wrapped their frostbitten, hypothermic bodies in dry flannel.

Once the gale had abated, Hanna used a sled to drag the men the 900 feet—all at a steep uphill grade—to his house. For two days, he and his wife nursed them until they were well enough to make the trip to Portland. On January 31, the keeper personally transported them nearly ten miles to the city.

Meanwhile, the storm enacted its full rage on the *Australia*, completely breaking her apart. Her timbers littered the shoreline for miles up and down the coast (most of this was hauled away and used for firewood by locals).

Captain Lewis's body washed up five days later, about a mile-and-a-half from the wreck site. Hanna transported the corpse to the coroner's office in Portland, and a funeral was held for the fallen captain two-and-a-half weeks after the wreck, on February 8, in Boothbay Harbor.

For his part in the valiant rescue, Hanna was recognized by the U.S. Life-Saving Service, receiving a gold medal—the agency's top honor—on April 25, 1885. And, interestingly, ten years later, upon his 53rd birthday, he was belatedly awarded a Congressional Medal of Honor by the U.S. War Department for his bravery in the Civil War during the siege of Port Hudson, Louisiana, in 1863.

In a precursor to his gallant rescue involving the *Australia*, the then twenty-one-year-old sergeant raced alone, across an open battlefield amidst enemy fire, to a water well. His body was strapped with a dozen empty canteens. After filling them, he ran back with the increased weight to deliver the water to his parched men.

Ever dedicated in his duties—whether during wartime or light-tending and life-saving—Hanna remains the only American to win both the nation's highest military and civilian honors for bravery. Hanna died at age seventy-nine in 1921 and he now maintains his well-earned rest at Mount Pleasant Cemetery in South Portland.

12

OWL'S HEAD

MYSTERIOUS WRECKAGE

"The sea is emotion incarnate. It loves, hates, and weeps. It defies all attempts to capture it with words and rejects all shackles. No matter what you say about it, there is always that which you can't."

—Christopher Paolini

From his prostrate position on the slick, ice-crusted rocks, the young deckhand squinted through the thrashing wind and the near-blinding flurry of sleet and snow.

If only he could reach the light off in the distance. But it seemed so far. Farther than his aching, frozen, bloodied body could handle. And his spot here where he collapsed was welcoming in its own way. He could just . . .

No.

That was hypothermia beginning to wrap its cold, deadly fingers around his wearied mind and body. He forced himself back to his brutal reality. He was colder than he had ever felt in his short life, his head was fuzzy, his body was becoming numb.

But he had to try.

Slowly, he raised himself to his hands and knees.

His hands were bloody from where he'd slashed and clawed himself out of the ice-crusted blanket before dragging his body over the side of the ship. He took one aching step after another, wobbly, hobbling, and leaving a trail of blood behind him that quickly congealed and froze in the arctic temperatures.

Almost there . . .

Almost there . . .

And suddenly he was bathed in warmth so shocking that it stung his skin and paralyzed his extremities.

He felt someone dragging him, agitatedly asking questions that his cold-stunted brain couldn't comprehend.

But finally, although his tongue felt like steel wool in his mouth, he forced himself to utter a plea: The mate . . . his bride-to-be—they were still out there, locked in a frozen embrace.

Rockland's Haunt

Mount the fifty-three steep steps to a narrow, rock-studded base barely wide enough for the nimblest of climbers, and then turn around to behold the glistening bay below. An impossibly blue sky is mirrored in a quintessentially cobalt Atlantic. Lobster boats and windjammers float calmly by the mounded humps of islands and the Camden hills. An American flag flutters in a breeze that, even on a pleasant day, threatens to steal the hats of the unsuspecting.

A stout lighthouse—thirty-feet tall and featuring the time-honored motif of white brick offset with black trim and capped with an ebony-colored lantern room—stands as the protector of this hill. Circling it are paths beaten down by visitors and lighthouse keepers. Hardy shrubs and menacing points of boulders as old as the ocean itself require careful footing.

It is a scene that, in 1891, prompted journalist Samuel Adams Drake to proclaim it "almost too beautiful to profane with speech when we are looking at it, impossible to find language to do it justice when memory would summon it before us again."

Yet standing on its promontory 100 feet above sea level, one can only imagine how forsaken and barren an outpost it could be when the sea and wind are disdainful in their relentless pounding and howling, and as brutally cold temperatures stiffen joints and harshly gnaw at any bit of exposed skin.

Keepers and their families have lived with this juxtaposition at Owl's Head Light since the tower was built in 1825. Located at the entrance to Rockland Harbor, the station is named for the outcropping it sits on, which some say has been sculpted by time to distinctively resemble the visage of the wise, wide-eyed bird. Others say it is a bastardized English translation of its original native name "Medadacut."

The area was the setting for fierce fighting between natives and would-be European settlers—including one instance in which an English captain used the Indians' tactics on themselves, brutally scalping them. Another time, in 1745, a ship was tricked ashore by natives; the captain's son, Thomas Sanders, was captured. His father sent a ransom of fifty pounds, but Thomas escaped, stealing his guard's gun and burying the ransom—which he eventually retrieved fifteen years later.

The light was deemed necessary in the early 1800s—and authorized by President John Quincy Adams—once locals began quarrying lime and a building boom commenced in the southern states.

One of the many examples of shipwrecks occurring along the shores below the lighthouse—and indeed among the luckier ones—was that of *The City of Portland*. Around 3:15 a.m. on May 8, 1884, the 1,000-ton vessel smashed into a shoal, running aground at Grindstone Ledge. Miraculously, its seventy passengers escaped injury and death—due largely to the fact that the wooden ship was "hard on the rocks" and all but immovable, affording all those aboard the time and opportunity to escape.

A much more mysterious instance involved the brig *Maine*, which departed on its first and last voyage in November 1844. Carrying a hull full of lime bound for New Orleans, the ship and its entire nine-person crew completely disappeared after passing by Owl's Head. Keeper Penley Haines was said to be the last to lay eyes on it as it sailed out of Rockland Harbor on the clear afternoon of November 9.

That was, until pieces of it turned up three years later. At that time, a passing boat dropped anchor in Rockland Harbor, carrying with it a mahogany chest, a ship's atlas, and navigation book that were all identified as belonging to the captain of the *Maine* and his mates.

When interrogated, the presiding mariner stammered ignorance about their origin, only offering the paltry breadcrumb of information that they were left behind by three Portuguese sailors who served on the boat for a time before jumping ship in Santa Cruz.

Could it be that the men had been involved in the *Maine*'s disappearance and feared capture? Or had the items just been "lucky" finds? Had the ship been dashed to pieces? Absconded by pirates? Lost in the rogue waves of the open sea?

The questions still linger.

But it was shipwreck in 1850, as trade and travel increased throughout Penobscot Bay, that served as the backdrop for one of the strangest stories involving Owl's Head.

The Frozen Lovers

It was just a few days before Christmas. A remarkable storm suddenly whipped through without warning, sending five vessels aground.

One of them, a small coasting schooner meandering through the area, had been moored off Jameson's Point not far from the bay's lighthouse. Its captain had made the trek into nearby Rockland, leaving three aboard: first mate Richard B. Ingraham, seaman Roger Elliott, and Lydia Dyer, Ingraham's bride-to-be.

When Mother Nature, in her ferocity, hurled up whirlwinds of ice, snow, and waves, the ship's moorings buckled, then snapped. Despite the sailors' efforts, it was pounded and smashed about like a toy, eventually getting pinned against the rocks at Owl's Head.

As the storm continued to jostle and bat at the stranded vessel, it quickly filled with water, although it didn't sink. Instead, giant waves tossed relentless spray across its bow, threatening to freeze its three trapped and terrified passengers to death.

Thinking quickly, the mate suggested they roll up in a blanket and lie together in the shelter of the stern, in the hopes that the icy water would provide a protective shell around the wool.

It did—but it became a tomb.

Arctic spray still flying, the three bundled together under their covering, which was soon encrusted with several inches of ice. The mate and his female companion succumbed to the cold, losing consciousness.

Believing that he was the only one alive, the deck mate contorted his body so that he could retrieve a small knife from his pocket. He then slashed at the frozen blanket with the blade; once he could see an opening, he beat, clawed, and ripped his way out, bloodying his hands.

Finally freed, he crawled over the side of the boat and made his way to the lighthouse off in the distance. He limped across a narrow bridge of rock that was exposed by low tide.

Lighthouse keeper Henry Achorn was astonished by the man's glaciated state. He quickly organized a rescue party of local men that rushed out to the wreck.

On the boat, they found the young lovers as they had been described, encased in ice, wrapped tightly in each other's arms.

They were presumed dead—but their rescuers didn't give up hope.

They laboriously dragged the frozen couple back to the lighthouse, where they worked away at their ice coffin with picks, chisels, and knives. They then bathed them in cold baths, slowly raising the temperature by dumping in buckets of increasingly warmer water. They also massaged them, and stretched out their lifeless limbs.

Remarkably, the woman started showing signs of life; she was revived, weary, exhausted, and injured as she was.

A little while later, her beau began to stir, opening his eyes and beckoning in slurred, halted speech, "What is all this? Where are we?"

They were rested, washed, and given water and bits of warm food.

Although it took several months, they both made a full recovery, and were married the following summer (and they eventually had four children together).

Meanwhile, Dyer never fully recovered, living with various ailments from the accident for the rest of his life. Perhaps understandably so, he never returned to sea. But as he lived out the rest of his days on the waterfront not far from Owl's Head, he never tired of regaling anyone with the story—and who could blame him?

It was a truly astonishing rescue—and, literally, a case of love put on ice.

13

LEISURE TURNED DEADLY

"And this terrifying enemy surfaced, as such enemies often do, in the seemingly most innocent, and unlikely, of places."

—*Little Shop of Horrors*

On August 6, 1899, what was to be a routine run for the Mount Desert Ferry boat *Sappho* turned into a deadly melee. Inexplicably, a gang plank gave way, sending two-hundred people tumbling into the cold waters of the harbor.

End-over-end, they knocked against, grabbed at, and were tangled up with one another as they fell fifteen feet into chilly waters. Arms and legs flailed helplessly; hands frantically grasped for any means of salvation. The air was filled with the chaotic chorus of shrieks, cries, and panicked splashing.

The would-be passengers of the Mount Desert Ferry were trapped, penned in on all sides by the pilings of the dock and the boat. Many of the men, women, and children were unable to swim, and quickly tired themselves with their feverish exertions. They clung to one another as they waited for a rescue that might never come. Many more continued their thrashings, or hysterically grabbed ahold of adjacent bodies in futile attempts to use them as life preservers, or climbed atop them as if they were buoys (in the process, ultimately dooming both due to the combined weight).

Before long, many slipped below the surface and drowned—having been injured or knocked unconscious during the fall, having exhausted themselves in their frenzy for survival, or having been dragged or yanked underwater by fellow hapless victims. Seventeen men, women, and children ultimately perished.

The would-be passengers were members of an excursion party from Bangor and other points on the Maine Central Railroad line, which operated its Bar Harbor Express Train—known by the colloquialism of the time as a "crack-train" due to its speed—northwards from New York City and Boston. Notably, the fleet of the Northeast Atlantic Squadron—fresh off a victory in the Spanish American War—was visiting Bar Harbor, where parades, picnics, and other festivities had been planned.

As was practice, guests and luggage detrained and queued up to board the local ferry steamer for the short trip to their summer destination. The *Sappho* (named for a female lyrical poet of Ancient Greece) was docked, as per usual, at Ferry Point in Hancock, about eight miles across the bay from Bar Harbor. The 275-ton, 140-foot-long boat and dock were connected by a wooden boarding ramp equipped with a series of chains and counterweights that could shift with the tide and currents—thus aligning them no matter the conditions.

That Sunday morning, no doubt in pleasant company and eagerly anticipating their leisure time, passengers began gathering on the gangplank to board the ferry. Rumors had circulated that the *Sappho* was too small to accommodate everyone, so many of the passengers had rushed there. Too late, ferry officials realized that they were too many people to accommodate in one trip. Soon, the slip was crammed with people, and was slanting downwards at a roughly twenty-five-degree angle.

Then, all of a sudden, there was a very loud crack—as sound described by some witnesses "as if from a cannon"—and the structure collapsed.

Dumped into waters that, no matter the time of year, are characteristically frigid, the passengers struggled and flailed for several minutes, "while more than a hundred excursionists above on the deck looked on, stupefied, and failing at first to realize the enormity of the tragedy they were witnessing," as reported by the *New York Times*.

Understandably, "a mass panic ensued," as the victims were shut in on all sides and had no avenue of escape. Rescue was delayed due to this circumstance, as well, as it was impossible to navigate into the area with small boats. Ropes and life preservers were thrown down, and many people were pulled out of the water "with great difficulty" by sheer man (and woman) power. Several of those tugged free were unconscious and near death.

The steamer *Cymbria*, also owned by the Maine Central Railroad, was quickly dispatched from Bar Harbor, four doctors aboard. Survivors needing immediate medical attention were taken to Hotel Bluffs nearby, where doctors had set up emergency facilities.

The less fortunate ones, however, were taken to the freight house at the dock, which was used as a temporary morgue. The identified bodies were then removed by families and friends. By noontime, twenty bodies had been assembled there, including three that had died after being pulled from the water. This made for an "appalling death toll," the *Times* lamented, and an impaneled jury performed an inquest, although it is unclear what the results were or whether any charges were filed.

In any case, the disaster involving the Mount Desert Ferry remains one of the greatest losses of civilian life in Maine maritime history.

Sometimes—oftentimes—it is when we least expect it that tragedy strikes us broadside. Such was the case for those unsuspecting ferry-riders on that August morning of 1899—and those about the *Don* forty years later. The pleasure craft and its more than three dozen excursionists simply disappeared in the waters of Casco Bay in the summer of

1941, and the mystery of its fate (and whereabouts) still bewilders all these decades later.

The *Don*: A Confounding Casualty of Casco Bay

It was to be a laid-back excursion to Monhegan Island, where a community clambake welcoming more than three dozen people had been organized by Albert Melanson of the Rumford Falls Trust Company. The journey to the island from Dyer's Cove in East Harpswell was set to depart at 7 a.m. on Sunday, June 29, 1941. The revelers were to be carried the twenty-three miles—an over-water trip of about two hours and forty-five minutes—aboard the 44-foot cabin cruiser the *Don*.

Perhaps a bad omen from the start, unspecified delays postponed the trip for two-and-a-half hours. Nevertheless, spirits were high as friends and family members assembled at the cove, many after attending church together in Rumford. Melanson had held a clambake on the island the previous summer, and he wrote to Captain Paul Johnson that "the gang" had all enjoyed the cruise and had talked about it all winter long. Many attending this year's repeat rendezvous were employees of the Oxford Paper Mill in Rumford, and there were several family groups—including the Melansons; he brought along his brother and his two teenage sons. Johnson also looked forward to the cruise; he liked the party and enjoyed their fun-loving company.

With the tide low, a rowboat ferried passengers back and forth to the leisure craft, where they situated themselves in either the cabin or the top deck. Roughly three-dozen passengers, including Johnson, were aboard. Finally, at 9:30, the *Don* headed out of the cove. Joseph Bernier, who partnered with Johnson to take out fishing and sailing parties, watched as it departed, and recalled seeing a young woman tossing a beach ball on its deck.

The ship headed out six miles across the bay channel, soon landing near Cape Small at West Point. Many disembarked, as was custom, to stretch their legs and peruse the shelves of Reed's General Store. This included Johnson, who purchased potatoes and onions to make a chowder aboard. Passengers, meanwhile, purchased candy, ice cream, refreshments, and postcards that they immediately mailed.

These proved foreboding—jinxing, even—following the tragedy.

While twenty-year-old Beatrice Roach wrote innocently enough to her mother that she was "Feeling fine, not seasick. But there is still 30 more miles to go," her fellow passenger Leila Sanders sent a postcard to Mrs. Daniel Wight stating, "No casualties yet!"

Curiously, in a letter to Captain Johnson dated June 19, Melanson also made the hexing jest that, "One of the mermaids has made a bet with me that we couldn't reach Monhegan. Hope I don't lose out. Don't forget the water this trip. So barring a hurricane or an all-day pouring rain, we'll be there. So shiver my timbers till next Sunday, Your Pop-eyed mate."

Whatever cruel fate had in store for the *Don*, though, she continued on her way at least from this point in her journey—re-loaded with her passengers, she headed out the channel toward Monhegan. From there, she passed by Seguin Island Light, where she was spotted by second assistant keeper Maxwell A. Deshon, and was last seen by witnesses around 11:20 a.m. about a quarter-mile from Tom's Rocks (a shoal between Seguin and Boothbay Harbor).

And then she disappeared.

As the day progressed, the fair weather gave way to increased fog, thick haze, and heavy swells. As these conditions worsened and darkness began to fall, the family members of those aboard grew concerned. Some of them gathered at the cove, standing by cars whose owners would never return to claim them. Alice Dyer's home soon became an unofficial headquarters for family and friends.

By late Sunday night, with the ship still not showing up on the horizon, local fishermen and others began searching the fog-shrouded waters of Casco Bay. That search continued Monday in almost zero visibility due to continued haze.

Nothing turned up—and then the grave news came from Monhegan that the *Don* had never arrived at her final destination.

M.H. Seavey, of the Boothbay Harbor Coast Guard Station, performed a scouring search around Seguin Island, Damariscove, Bailey Island, Monhegan and its harbor, Pemaquid Point, and up the Sheepscot River to Bath.

Still nothing was found.

Loved ones and would-be rescuers held out hope that the cruiser was holed up at anchor in a harbor or cove to wait out the fog. Search parties formed and planned throughout the night to head out at dawn on Tuesday.

But then their worst fears were confirmed.

On Tuesday, two bodies were discovered off Bailey Island, and quickly identified as passengers of the *Don*. Over the course of the next several days, additional bodies were found floating throughout Casco Bay or washed up along its shores. The last body to be found was pulled out of the Atlantic a full two weeks after the group had set out for their seemingly benign clam bake excursion.

Twenty bodies were never recovered, and remain forever lost at sea.

Almost immediately, the media staked out Dyer's Cove, East Harpswell, and its environs, capturing stark images of recovered bodies wrapped in tarps, stricken family members, and perplexed policemen. Articles appeared in periodicals up and down the east coast, chronicled the daily events (or lack thereof), lamenting the civilian tragedy, and offering summary and speculation. Among some, the *Don* came to be known as the "jinx boat."

Amidst the growing frenzy of attention, the Maine State Police instructed the coroner to inspect the bodies for burns, abrasions, or other markings. Burns were not discovered, although the shoes on one of the bodies appeared to be slightly singed. Several of the bodies did have red spots and markings identified as "water burns," which can be caused by scalding water, as well as bruises that were deemed to be either postmortem or sustained immediately before death. The legs of some victims also appeared to have been attacked by dogfish or sharks (undoubtedly occurring while they were adrift following the *Don*'s demise).

Meanwhile, the circumstances in which Captain Johnson's body was recovered proved mystifying: Found near Pond Island Ledge, his clothing had either been washed away or stripped off prior to his death, and a keg attached to three fathom length of rope had been slipped over his waist and under his arms. That keg would normally have been used as a buoy for tuna fishing and was emblazoned with "Capt. P.R. Johnson, East Harpswell Maine."

Still, neither the conditions of any of the bodies, nor the locations of their recovery, offered any foregone conclusions. The only way to determine death would have been autopsies—but lacking consent from grieving family members, most causes were listed as "accidental drowning."

Along with the water-logged corpses, all manner of debris washed in, and locals were more than willing to turn in any and all items they found in hopes to aid investigations. Among the items collected was an awning similar to one on the *Don*; a piece of green wooden trim and some other charred bits of wood including a partially-burned wooden grate; a wooden spout with a bilge pump; a portion of a boat rail so singed that it broke into two pieces when hauled aboard; a thermos that seemed to have been exposed to extensive heat; a lobster buoy spindle etched with the name *Don*; and a pair of trousers, hats, and some scorched items of clothing.

Johnson's partner Bernier, later recalled seeing the beach ball—the one being carefreely tossed by the young woman as the ship sailed out—drifting along the ocean surface near Flat Ledge.

Notably, several watches washed ashore, all of them stopped around the same time—11:35, 11:40, 11:43, 11:45.

Most notably, of the forty brand new life preservers that had been aboard, just one was recovered: in new condition, never used, and folded in the same manner as it had been when received from the manufacturer.

Still, most of these items could not be definitively linked to the *Don*. And, much like the bodies, they offered no clue as to what had happened to her—or where her remains might be found.

Theories and Lasting Impacts

All this simply added fuel to the already swirling conflagration of speculation.

Namely, people talked about Johnson—and questioned the condition and reliability of his craft.

The forty-five-year-old veteran fisherman, lobsterman, and skipper was known by some as an adventurist who liked to travel the waters of Casco Bay during storms, and explore strange coves and rough channels. Still, they said, he knew how to handle a boat, he was intimately familiar with local waters, and he was a skilled mechanic experienced with motors.

With the excursion on June 29 being the *Don*'s first cruise of the year, Johnson had diligently checked the condition of the life jackets (which were brand new), charged the battery, and completed repairs to the gas tank. He had also taken a heavier anchor aboard, according to his partner Bernier. However, some pointed out that the captain had carelessly left his ship at its mooring—and fully exposed to the elements—for all of the preceding winter.

The ship, which had been built in Nova Scotia in 1936, had previously sunk at least two, if not three, times. The *Don* had been significantly altered over the years—including, most extensively, by Johnson. Johnson purchased the *Don* in 1940 and remodeled her to include a hunter cabin with glass windows. This task required raising both the bow and deck by a few feet each. Johnson spliced up all the oak timber for this himself, and also installed new floors and buffalo rails, while performing caulking, painting, and seam cementing.

Featuring a mahogany hull and heavy planking, the pleasure craft had a cockpit and seats to her rear that accommodated about a dozen passengers. Another twelve people or so could crowd into the engine room space, and yet another dozen into the cabin forward of the engine. The cabin was only equipped with one door, which was through the rear to the cockpit. There was also a toilet on board.

The many who weighed in following the wreck said that these changes caused the boat to have a very high bow that curved out and sat about seven feet above the water line. Some posited that this remodeling made the craft top-heavy and too narrow for her length—and thus easily prone to rolling. State Fisheries Warden John Stevens later attested to this very fact. Other witnesses who saw the *Don* on the morning of its last voyage also described a cabin loaded with passengers, their weight causing the craft's prow to pound heavily in the swells.

Meanwhile, the quarters around her gas tank and cookstove were tight (perhaps dangerously so). A brass pipe vent soldered to the 300-pound gas tank fit so snugly into a hole in the roof that there was hardly any play. Not far from this tank, in the forward part of the boat, a cast iron range had been installed. The tank and the range were separated by two partitions of unknown thickness or reliability.

Some, then, surmised that the *Don* had gone down in an explosion due to problems with the tank, or due to a gas leak that spilled gasoline into the bilge, filled the cabin with fumes, and ignited into flame when Johnson lit the cookstove to make his chowder. Warden Stevens didn't rule this out as a possibility; he recalled being on the boat not long before its fateful voyage, and described a smell of gasoline so strong that he quickly tossed his lit cigar into the ocean.

Others, though, refuted this theory, pointing to the situation with the life jackets—only one had been found. They argued that, had there been an explosion, life jackets (along with other debris) would have been scattered everywhere across the water and along the shoreline.

Then there was the situation with the recovered bodies. The absence of any significant markings or injuries, as well as the fact that they floated so soon after the tragedy, seems to refute deaths by drowning or explosion. As Stacy L. Welner explains in her comprehensive account, *Tragedy in Casco Bay*, drowned bodies typically sink immediately, and it takes eight to ten days before the internal gasses that develop during composition build up enough to send them back up to the surface. This process, however, can be impacted by the type of water (salt vs. fresh) as well as its temperature.

The recovery of the body of thirty-five-year-old Elizabeth P. Howard would seem to support this—described by family members and friends as being an "outdoor enthusiast and excellent swimmer"—as would the body of Captain Johnson. The fact that he had secured a keg to himself led some to believe that he may have been using it as a safety buoy as he repeatedly dove to save trapped passengers as the ship went down. Bernier likewise described him as a strong swimmer who would "rather swim a mile than to row it."

While some held fast to the explosion hypothesis—and others clung to more far-fetched conspiracy theories involving U-Boat attacks, a deliberate sinking to collect insurance money, even a broken, roving mine that worked its way down the coast from Halifax Harbor before accidentally colliding with the *Don*—the prevailing opinion was that the craft had rolled. This sudden capsizing was due to its inherent instability and the added weight of the passengers. The accident probably occurred after it was caught in a groundswell or struck a submerged ledge. The vessel then rapidly sank. The impact would have likely knocked many passengers unconscious, immediately drowning some, and trapping the remainder inside.

This was the official decision, following an investigation by a Maine State Board of Inquiry appointed by Governor Sumner Sewall. Testimony took place in the federal building in Portland on July 24 and 25, 1941. Those called to testify included Johnson's partner Bernier, as well as the Seguin Island lightkeeper Deshon, storekeeper Alton P. Reed, Captain Johnson's housekeeper, a former *Don* deckhand, and several local fishermen and boat builders. Investigators considered weather and temperature records, and also analyzed blueprints of the boat, numerous photographs, and artist renderings depicting passenger locations that morning.

Still, Johnson was in full compliance with the boating laws of the time: Because it was registered as a pleasure craft, the *Don* did not require a license, nor inspection prior to use, and it could legally carry passengers, so long as there were enough life jackets on board (which there were) and the boat was registered with the Steamboat Inspection Department (which it was).

So if any sense of hope, meaning, or silver lining can be drawn from the tragedy, this would be it. Taking into account that the Don was in full compliance—yet still resulted in the loss of roughly three dozen lives—the Board recommended to the Secretary of Commerce that all such vessels undergo inspection or examination as a means to help protect the public. Notably, they urged that this inspection should help determine the craft's stability. They also recommended that a small dinghy or rowboat be placed on board or towed astern at all times that a vessel of the *Don*'s type was underway; that stoves for cooking or heating be prohibited from the compartment containing the main gasoline or diesel engine or any spaces adjoining it; that there be a limit on the number of passengers allowed to be carried; and that lifesaving equipment be examined and marked.

Furthermore, they recommended every motorboat carrying passengers for hire should be inspected for its seaworthiness and equipment, and that maximum number should be designated by a certificate issued by local inspectors. Any violation of the foregoing, according to the Board, "shall be considered as operating in a reckless or negligent manner."

Ultimately, though, questions remain about where exactly the fated ship met her final end.

The Board's official opinion—informed by local officials and fishermen familiar with the tides—was that the ship and its passengers perished shortly after leaving the West Point Shore and after being sighted by the Seguin lightkeeper. This leaves much up for interpretation—as does the fact that most of the bodies were discovered between Bailey Island and Ragged Island. Did the *Don* encounter disaster in the inner bay? Near Bailey Island? At Mark Island Ledges?

Even if the remnants of the wreck churn up out of the Atlantic all these years later, we will never know for sure. Only the ocean, and her victims, know their final truth.

14

THE LAST IN A CLASS

WASHINGTON B. THOMAS

"Beauty is fading, nor is fortune stable; sooner or later death comes to all."

—Propertius

In the brief period they ruled the seas, they were magnificent beauties to behold: massive yet elegant, billowing at full-sail, prow proudly raised against the waves, a quintessential image of sail.

The aptly-named "great schooners" were four-masted—and the ever-rarer five and six-masted—wooden sailing vessels that transported large-bulk cargoes up and down the east coast at the close of the nineteenth and the opening of the twentieth centuries.

Now considered the last technical achievement of wooden shipbuilders, they emerged to meet demand for coastwise trade amidst foreign competition that specialized in long, deepwater voyages. Averaging three-hundred feet long and weighing more than 3,500 tons, they carried local products such as lumber and cordwood, ice, hay, dried fish and potatoes to southern ports; then returned with such goods as coal, southern pine lumber, fertilizer, or turpentine.

Maine shipbuilders, especially, excelled at turning out the impressive vessels. In fact, the first four-masted schooner was the *William L. White*, built in 1880 by Goss, Sawyer, & Packard of Bath. All told, Maine craftsmen produced 327 of the 458 four-masted schooners, fifty-three of the fifty-seven five-masted schooners, and all ten of the six-masted schooners.

In the half-century or so that they were employed in their duties, the vessels were considered more cost-effective and better suited for short-haul routes than the prevailing square-rigged vessels of the day. This was due largely to their use of "fore-and-aft" rigs that proved superior in variable, changing weather conditions and smoother, calmer coastal waters; as such, they required a much smaller crew. Despite their size, they could also be built at a lower cost. (Of course, few traditional sailing vessels could compete with the steamers, barges and railroads that were to arrive with the new century.)

While some called these masted schooners "the most weatherly and economical sailing vessels in the world," one of their massive shortcomings was their inability to react quickly in emergencies.

This is where the *Washington B. Thomas* sails (briefly, and fatedly) into the story.

Built by the Washburn Brothers of Thomaston, the nearly 287-foot-long, forty-eight-and-a-half-foot-wide schooner was launched on April 11, 1903, and was the largest vessel of any description ever crafted in Thomaston. Built for Captain William J. Lermond, the grand ship featured 3,500 yards of sail when fully rigged, and each of her five masts was made from a single, 115-foot stick of Oregon pine. From these masts, in turn, rose fifty-seven-foot topmasts.

Photographs taken during the latter stages of her construction and "fitting out" depict her true enormity and majesty. In one, looking back from her bow toward her stern, her deck stretches far beyond the periphery of sight; all the while, workers on either side of her massive masts busy themselves with their duties. In another, her full length and height dominate the entire frame—not to mention Thomaston Harbor—her masts reaching high into the sky, fully-rigged and ready. Photographers also captured Lermond (or "Captain Bill," as he was less-formally known) in his elaborately-decorated cabin with his wife and son. As was the grim Victorian fashion, the three sit stoically, dressed in their best dark-colored clothing, in a space featuring marbled floors and heavy paneled doors, furnished with heavy chairs, and decked out with a chandelier, a portrait, and a small phonograph machine.

Lermond was experienced with more than 40 years at sea, most profitably shuttling lumber from New Brunswick to Great Britain, and coal from Great Britain to the Mediterranean. In the spring of 1903, he performed a series of so-called shakedown runs in the *Thomas* to Newport News, Virginia—meant to work the literal and figurative kinks out—before returning to Thomaston.

It was then that Lermond brought aboard his new, young wife—the former Hattie Mae Winchenbach. In what many superstitious sailors would consider a bad omen, it was her first time at sea. But, having recently remarried following the death of his first wife, the captain was in high spirits, and intended for the voyage to be a coastwide vacation and honeymoon, as well as a business trip. He also brought along his son, Bowdoin.

It would prove an abbreviated celebration, however—as well as the ship's last, catastrophic excursion.

Carrying 4,226 tons of soft coal for Portland-based Randall & McAllister Company, the *Thomas* sailed out of its home port for the last time on May 26, headed once again for Newport News. Once it delivered its cargo, it sailed back for Maine on June 3, arriving off the Isles of Shoals (an island chain zig-zagging the Maine-New Hampshire maritime border) around noon on June 11.

Sailing on into the afternoon, Lermond began to encounter light onshore breezes and dense fog, and he grew leery of taking the ship near Portland Harbor in such conditions. Around 7 p.m., just as his crew sighted Richmond Island off Cape Elizabeth, thick, penetrating fog tumbled in over the water, nearly eliminating visibility. The captain decided to tack toward shore, then relieved his sails and dropped his starboard anchor in about nineteen fathoms (115 feet) of water. By this time, the Thomas *was* about three miles equidistant from Richmond Island and the Cape Elizabeth lightship.

And then, as the ship sat otherwise unperturbed at anchor, it began to rain. Precipitation grew ever-steadier, descending with the night. With it, the fog thickened, becoming ever more tangible, onshore winds whipped up and the seas followed suit, mounting larger and larger waves. Finally, gale force winds joined in, purportedly gusting up to fifty miles an hour.

Faced with this litany of forces, the *Thomas* suddenly "jumped"—or dragged her anchor. With the robust winds and heavy seas unceasing, and visual clarity still at zero, Lermond was concerned the ship might be moving dangerously closer to shore. He ordered the port anchor dropped.

Still, the ship continued to drag.

In what would seem a contradictory measure, the captain then had the crew hoist the *Thomas*'s sails in an attempt to keep the vessel's head to the wind, while also relieving strain on her anchors. But after doing so—the ship's sails thus billowing, flapping, and creaking with the strain—the crew discovered that her starboard anchor had snapped free, and, despite their efforts, they were unable to release her port anchor.

Then, sometime after 11 p.m., the ship abruptly jounced; it had hit a submerged ledge. It then continued on an erratic drift—and straight toward voracious-looking shoals that until then had been cloaked by fog and sea. Her crew and captain helpless to prevent it, the *Thomas* struck the shoals amidships (at her center); the sea than lifted the prone, damaged schooner, throwing her angrily against an offshore reef, destroying her undersides. Her forward portion now lay atop an extensive ledge formation that runs off the northeastern end of Stratton Island, a low, flat, twenty-acre outcropping that sits between Richmond and Wood islands. While adrift, she had traveled downwind more than six miles.

Giant waves pummeled the ship, forcing it ever more firmly upon the rocks. Finally, it was lodged firm; the front end of the ship was stuck full on the rocks, while its stern hung suspended—and tilted downward—in deep water. Quickly, seas began to pour into exposed, ripped-open portions of the ship.

Acknowledging his defeat to the mighty sea, Lermond ordered his men to save themselves; to escape the rising waters as the ship sank, the crew began climbing up upon the booms and into the rigging.

The captain then frantically went in search of his wife, who had been down in the cabin when the ship smacked into the shoals.

He found her there, hysterical, and attempted to calm her and coax her to the deck. But the sea then tossed up another indomitable wave that caved in the bulkhead, smashed the cabin's skylights, and knocked down a partition that struck the distraught Hattie Mae in the head, knocking her unconscious. The captain furiously searched for his wife amidst the floating labyrinth of debris—smashed-up portions of hull, broken furniture, shards of glass from the windows and chandelier—but her skull had been crushed by the wooden structure, and she had promptly drowned.

Throughout the night, the sea continued its battering. The ship's stern portion, which had for a time retained its relatively upright position, first began to sink, then was wrested free and beaten ashore. The load of coal that had been in the hold of the ship was released in a torrent into the ocean.

When daylight finally began its ascent, fog still presided, but the crew could make out the outline of the reef—as well as, just a few hundred feet southeast, the island.

And likewise. Early Saturday morning, Stratton's inhabitants—a caretaker and two workers who tended several acres of farmland—spotted the *Thomas* lying in her death throes on the rocks. Still, they were only able to watch helplessly; according to the official report from the U.S. Life-Saving Service, they "could not afford any aid, neither having a suitable boat nor men to man one; neither, on account of the fog, could they signal the mainland."

Emboldened by the daylight, crewmembers worked their way down from their perches in the rigging and picked about the detritus; they were able to recover bread and water, and gathered enough scraps for a makeshift shelter. Their movement proved increasingly difficult, however, as the ship, lightened from its heavy load of coal, now constantly swayed back and forth with the wind and rolling tide.

Other observers also saw the wreckage, and two men even attempted rescue in a dory, but were unable to follow through due to the incessantly rough seas. Attempts were made to call aid, but lines were down due to the storm. Finally, word reached Sumner N. Dyer, keeper of Cape Elizabeth Two Lights. As it was the summer, and the station was closed, he was alone; he quickly gathered up gear and summoned a group of local men, who loaded the station's lifeboat onto a wheeled contraption. After transporting the boat overland nineteen miles to Prouts Neck in Scarborough, they cast off into the sea at 6:45 p.m.

Despite still unabated fog and high seas, Dyer was able to bring the lifeboat safely alongside the desperate vessel. After several attempts, he was then able to land a thrown line on the wreck. This each man then tied around himself before jumping overboard and being pulled roughly sixty feet to the safety of the rescue boat. Nine were saved this way, including Bowdoin and another boy, until the rescue boat was full and the day (not to mention the weather) was failing.

The remaining five on board the *Thomas*—one with a broken leg, another with a broken arm, and Lermond himself battered and emotionally broken following his attempts to save his wife—were confident that the remaining portion of their vessel would survive for several hours until the rescue boat could return.

When it did, at 3 a.m., Dyer was able to position his dory directly beneath the schooner's port side, allowing the remaining five survivors to be lowered, rather than painstakingly dragged, to their salvation. Lermond, as befitting of a captain, was the last to leave; he cast off the lifeboat's line before sliding down a piece of standing rigging draped over the side of his defeated ship.

The captain was also the most seriously injured: He had severe scalp lacerations, nasty bruises covered his entire body, his feet and legs that were "parboiled" due to extended immersion in water, and he was experiencing excruciating back and chest pains. Not to mention the extreme agony he was feeling over the loss of his new bride and his magnificent ship.

As he and his men were taken away to receive medical attention and bedrest, the ship continued to break apart. Its wreckage washed ashore all along Saco Bay and Old Orchard Beach—bulwarks, railings, rigging, doors, life preservers, as well as a trunk containing several items, including calling cards imprinted with "Mrs. W.J. Lermond."

Never to come calling again, Hattie Mae's body finally washed ashore at Camp Ellis, about a quarter-mile north of the mouth of the Saco River. She was discovered at 11:30 a.m. on Sunday, just a day-and-a-half after the ship's fatal collision.

Within just a couple of weeks, wreckers had stripped nearly everything of value from the *Thomas*, including her engine and windlass. By that time, just two of the masts remained on the ship, whose halved, paralyzed, deteriorated hulk proved a pitiful sight out on the rocks. Those masts, too, were finally stripped (they were worth a valuable $500 each) and, over time, the remnants of the *Thomas* were slowly devoured.

Eventually, all that was left of the *Thomas* were the ribs that once held her superstructure together. For many years, these could be seen poking up through the sand at low tide—a mere remnant of her past grandeur, and a pitiful reminder of the "great schooners" bygone era.

15

THE USS *EAGLE 56*

A STEALTH ENEMY VICTORY

"Let your plans be dark and impenetrable as night, and when you move, fall like a thunderbolt."

—Sun Tzu

Completely covert, moving undetected and silent beneath the waves, the submarine closed in.

Its enemy blissfully unaware of its presence, the U-Boat set its sights. And fired.

The hit was direct, and fatal. The target, the U.S. Navy vessel USS *Eagle 56*, was immediately ripped in half. Within minutes, it sank. Nearly all of its crew were killed.

Its task completed, the German submarine *U-853*—a giant, silent beast of man's making—promptly disappeared back into the icy, black depths from whence it came.

On April 23, 1945, the *Eagle 56*, a training ship engaged in routine duties in Portland Harbor, was struck and destroyed by the *U-853*, a

German U-Boat that for weeks had clandestinely prowled the waters off the east coast. Resulting in forty-nine deaths, it was the greatest loss of life in any incident in New England waters during World War II.

Yet the full truth of the tragedy would not be revealed for more than fifty years—making it, ultimately and perhaps unwittingly, an ever more decisive enemy victory. What's more, despite numerous efforts to locate it, the fallen ship would remain vexingly hidden below the Atlantic until its discovery by recreational divers in June 2018.

Deceptive Depths

The *Eagle 56* was of a class of Navy vessels developed during World War I; they were patrol craft made to be compact and maneuverable. Built by the Ford Motor Company under the direction of the legendary Henry Ford himself, the 200-foot-long, steel-hulled ships were named after an editorial in the *Washington Post* that called for "an eagle to scour the seas and pounce upon and destroy every German submarine." The first of the sixty Eagle ships was launched in July 1918, just four months to the day before the signing of the November 11 armistice that ended the war.

Due to the timing and the fact that they were square-built slow and therefore not good sub-chasers, none of the ships saw action in World War II. Most were transferred to the U.S. Coast Guard, others became aircraft tenders, and eight of them were used in service in World War II, humankind's bloodiest, most horrific, battle against itself.

For her part, the *Eagle 56* (the fifth-to-the-last in the Eagle series) launched on August 15, 1919, on the Detroit River. She was used as a Naval Reserve training ship for the majority of her career, notably for sonar operations and in the development of antisubmarine torpedoes. She was involved in two rescues during the early years of World War II, including that of the USS *Jacob Jones* off Cape May, New Jersey, which was torpedoed in February 1942 by the German submarine *U-578*.

The *Eagle 56* arrived to her final port, the Naval Air Station Brunswick, on June 28, 1944, mere weeks after many thousands of allied troops had stormed and gained the blood-stained beaches of Normandy. Portland and its environs were busy throughout the war, with many tens of thousands of locals employed at prolific shipyards.

Captained by Lieutenant Commander James G. Early, the *Eagle 56*'s primary job was to tow a target float into, and out of, the waters of Cape Elizabeth. This target was used for practice by navy and marine bomber pilots, many of whom had seen action in both the Pacific and North American theaters.

Due to the timing and circumstances, Maine's waters were considered a relatively safe haven. Earlier in the raging conflict, German U-boats were well-known to be roaming waters up and down the Atlantic coast—between January and August 1942, for instance, they had sunk more than 600 American military and merchant vessels in a time that German commanders grotesquely referred to as the "Great American Turkey Shoot." The U.S. military had been slow to respond to these attacks, and many witnesses later reported that they were issued gag orders.

But thanks to stepped-up military production, success in breaking German codes, widespread military blackouts, convoy missions, and allied successes throughout Europe, the threat of attack was minimal.

Or so it was incorrectly, fatally, perceived.

Thus enters the *U-853*. Commanded by twenty-four-year-old Helmut Frömsdorf, and with a crew of fifty-five men, the submarine slipped undetected into the Gulf of Maine in 1945. At first, it had been identified and tracked in Washington, D.C., but such tracking grew difficult—then petered out—as the sub sent and received fewer communications amidst increasing Germans losses in Europe.

It was with this enemy ship lurking that the *Eagle 56* headed out on the morning of Monday, April 23, its crew of sixty-two officers and seamen performing their regular, routine duty of towing the target buoy out beyond Cape Elizabeth.

A little past noon, the *U-853* drew within 600 yards of the patrol vessel as it sat three miles offshore. It was an easy mark, and Frömsdorf readily took the opportunity. In short order, the sub fired a torpedo that ripped into the *Eagle 56* on her starboard side.

With a rending explosion, the ship broke in two. The resulting geyser of water was said to be two-hundred feet high, and purportedly could be seen from as far as Portland Head Light. The shock of the impact was also plainly heard from miles away.

All the men on the bridge and nearly all the men below deck in the bow section were killed, most likely instantaneously. Those who could save themselves did, leaping into waves made turbulent by the explosion and the resultant suction from the rapidly-sinking *Eagle 56*. Engineering officer John Scagnelli was the only man who escaped the bow section alive. He was knocked from the bunk in his cabin and suffered a deep scalp wound, recalling later that, "I was thrown just as if someone had picked me up and tossed me."

He and a handful of other survivors tread water or held fast to debris such as target buoys, barrels and food cases, watching helplessly, and with horror, as the bow sank below the surface with their fellow crewmembers inside. As they struggled to comprehend what had happened, several of these survivors recalled seeing the dark shape of a submarine tower rising out of the sea, then disappearing out of sight. It bore the insignia of a yellow shield with a red horse, which the German crew had painted on the *U-853* when they nicknamed her der Seiltänzer, or "the Tightrope Walker."

Twenty minutes after the blast, and with the besieged vessel all but consumed by the sea, crew members from the destroyer USS *Selfridge* began pulling the now hypothermic men out of the water. However, two more were inadvertently killed when the *Selfridge* started its engines in response to sharp sonar echoes—strong indication that a U-Boat was in the vicinity.

Of the sixty-two-man crew, only thirteen escaped; the *U-853* attack had succeeded in killing forty-nine men.

Still, it was the aftermath of the tragedy that some considered even more troublesome.

When initially notified of the deaths, families of the victims were given scant details—most were told simply that the men had been lost at sea.

Meanwhile, a U.S. Navy court of inquiry quickly convened on April 26, and pronounced its findings six days later. Despite testimony from victims and witnesses, Judge Advocate Norman Kaufmann stated that, "the only plausible conclusion . . . is that the explosion in this case was in the boiler. There was no fire, smoke, flame, or flying debris such as would have been present had the ship been torpedoed."

Furthermore, nothing about the explosion appeared in newspapers until May 9—more than two weeks later—due to the wartime censorship in effect. The stories that then ran reiterated the court of inquiry's assertion that the sinking was the result of a boiler explosion.

Meanwhile, as all of this was happening, the *U-853* got her due: Early in the evening of May 5, the sub fired a torpedo at the SS *Black Point* as the cargo ship was cruising along the Rhode Island coast to Boston with a hold full of 8,000 tons of coal. This attack came despite orders that very day by German head of state Karl Donitz that all U-Boats cease offensive operations and return to their bases. The torpedo blast blew off the stern of the 368-foot vessel, sinking her within fifteen minutes and killing twelve men aboard (she was crewed with forty-one merchant seamen and five armed guards). The *Black Point* was the last U.S.-flagged merchant ship lost in World War II.

Quickly, ten American ships descended, and a "hunter-killer" group of four warships gave chase during an intense, sixteen-hour attack. As the submarine alternately attempted to flee and hide by lying still, the "hunter-killers" bombarded the enemy vessel with rocket bombs, depth charges and "hedgehogs" (forward-throwing anti-submarine weapons) that finally broke through the U-Boat's hull. Her demise was confirmed when dispatchers spotted her badly-damaged hulk sunken to the ocean floor, filled with dead bodies. The wreck still lies there today, and is an active dive site—albeit a treacherous one. Today it is marked with signs warning: "DANGER—Unexploded depth charge May 1945."

In the weeks, months, and years following the attack on the *Eagle 56*, conjecture and conspiracy theories abounded. Most believed that local navy officials were embarrassed that an enemy ship had penetrated so close to Portland's harbor, and didn't want the public to know that

U-boats were still operating in New England waters—and perhaps even more so, feared court-martialing for losing a ship so close to shore when Germany was on the verge of surrender.

Even so, the court of inquiry's findings remained the official conclusion of record.

That was until more than a half-century later in 1998. This was when Massachusetts lawyer Paul Lawton took an interest in, and began investigating, the strange circumstances surrounding the *Eagle 56*'s sinking. An amateur historian with a strong interest in German U-Boats—and an innate strength in research—he requested the official records from the U.S. Navy but was informed that they were "presumed lost." In 1999, with assistance from retired navy captain Edward J. Melanson, these "lost" records were obtained. At this point, his dogged interest in the case gained the interest of then South Boston state representative Joseph Moakley.

In 2000, at Lawton's, Melanson's, and Moakley's insistence, the Naval Historical Center agreed to reexamine the case. A few months later, archivist Bernard Cavalcante determined that the *Eagle 56* had been sunk "by enemy action," and she recommended that the survivors be awarded Purple Heart medals. In late 2001, the Secretary of the Navy concurred, and a year later, in a ceremony aboard the USS *Salem* in southeastern Massachusetts, these distinctive medals were given out. Most were awarded posthumously to relatives, finally relieved to know the true nature of their loss.

And there, it would seem, the story bears its conclusion.

However, its dramatic denouement unspools ever further.

In June 2019, the wreck of the *Eagle 56* was reported found—nearly five miles offshore from Cape Elizabeth, three-hundred feet below the waves. Its watery resting place, never before seen by human eyes and unperturbed for more than seventy years, was discovered by a civilian team of divers following years of painstaking research.

Technical diver Ryan King described his first encounter with the site: Hundreds of feet down, in frigid, forty-degree waters with visibility less than five feet, suddenly, "out of the gloom, comes this giant wall of steel," he told the Maine Public Broadcasting Network (MPBN). "It was absolutely awe-inspiring."

King and his Nomad Exploration Team executed the exhaustive search along with Garry Kozak, a commercial diver and expert in the use of side-scan sonar, and documentary filmmaker Kirk Wolfinger. Throughout their scrutiny of Portland waters, they applied sonar technology and a magnetometer—which measures magnetic forces—scoured topography scans and GPS coordinates, and studied and developed all manner of charts, maps, weather, and historical data.

Beyond the inherent pitfalls and challenges due to the ocean's vast, turbulent, concealing nature, the *Eagle 56* proved so perplexing a find because of its depth at 300 feet, the area's confusing, irregular topography, as well as the fact that it had been split in half upon impact—those two segments now sit about 350 feet apart on the ocean floor. Likewise, because the Atlantic is littered with debris—and so much of it iron—"it was like looking for a needle in a haystack full of needles," Wolfinger told MPBN.

After definitively identifying the wreck themselves, the search team sought—and quickly received—official agreement from the Navy that it was, indeed, the remains of the *Eagle 56*. Over the ensuing weeks and months, they returned to the site fifteen to twenty times, according to King, and thus chronicled the momentous discovery and survey of the wreckage for the Smithsonian documentary, *The Hunt for Eagle 56*, which Wolfinger produced and directed. During those dives, they captured footage of the two sprawling remnants of the hull, including artifacts such as depth charges and an intact, sixteen-foot deck-mounted gun.

Most notable, though, was their location of the downed ship's boilers—which were fully intact, ultimately providing definitive proof that they were not the culprit in the *Eagle 56*'s sinking.

Now considered a war grave, the wreck site is federally protected. Even so, as Wolfinger notes, it has vast and valuable implications for history, anthropology, and forensics (potentially providing further insight into how and why ships sink), not to mention even more specialized areas of study such as dendrochronology (the analysis of tree rings and wood).

"This is time, frozen," said Wolfinger. "Whatever happened when this ship went down, it's all right here."

So they say, the truth always eventually presents itself—even if it takes persistent time and patience, not to mention some coaxing of the reluctant, cloaking embrace of the sea.

A Concrete Ship?

Another unusual—yet not quite so enduringly irksome—story of a military ship's demise in Maine waters is that of the SS *Polias*.

Much like the *Eagle 56*, she was built in the waning months of World War I as part of a pilot project approved by President Woodrow Wilson. The unique endeavor called for the building of twenty-four ships from concrete.

While it might seem a foolhardy proposition, the U.S. was dealing with a critical lack of merchant cargo vessels—during World War I, the country's merchant fleet ranked a mere twentieth in the world—at the same time that steel was becoming in short supply (and thus ever-more expensive). Wilson received intelligence that concrete ships were more economically and structurally sound, requiring one-third of the steel as that of an ordinary steamship.

Ultimately, only twelve of the ships were constructed, the *Polias* being the first, and one of the prototypes—although she was not launched until a month after the war closed, in December 1918. Crafted of a mixture of cement, sand and gravel, her shell averaged five inches in thickness, and when fully reinforced, decked and fitted, the 267-foot vessel weighed 2,564 gross tons.

In short time, the concrete fleet proved heavy and uneconomical; on average, they were a whopping 39 percent heavier, and carried 5 percent less cargo. One-time *Polias* crewmember Barney Burnett, for example, recalled "how stiff" the concrete ship was. "She never rose to the sea, but just plowed through it rigidly," he said. "She was a war emergency vessel that I felt was dangerous."

Indeed, the ship (named after the ancient Greek goddess associated with wisdom, warfare, and handicraft) was only in service for less than a year-and-a-half, until the combination of a great New England gale and her heavy bulk permanently stranded her off the Maine coast.

Captained by Richard T. Coughlan, she was used to shuttle coal from Virginia to midcoast paper mills.

It was on this regular trek that, on February 2, 1920, she ran into intense, raging weather off the coast of Port Clyde.

The winter at the turn of the decade—1919 into 1920—has been described as one of the most severe of the twentieth century. Due to benumbing cold and record snowfall, some harbors and their entrances were completely iced over, coastal shipping lanes were clogged with ice floes, and drifts in coastal cities such as Portland reached second-story windows. As a result, maritime activity was restricted, and Coast Guard cutters and steam tugs worked side-by-side to clear ice-choked waterways. With lines down for extended periods nearly everywhere, communication was sparse and difficult.

The *Polias*, sailing on just her fifth voyage with a crew of thirty-eight aboard, had begun the southward trek from Searsport to Norfolk. The weather conditions were the worst Captain Coughlan had ever seen; it was fiercely cold, the seas were fervent, and unpredictable snow squalls blotted out visibility, including the lighthouse beams of Two Bush Island, Whitehead, and Monhegan Island. Many channel buoys had also been sheathed in ice and were difficult to locate.

As she proceeded down West Penobscot Bay around 6 p.m., the *Polias* suddenly ground her hull along the northern end of Old Cilley Ledge, about five miles south of Port Clyde. After the jarring, grating impact, she was stuck securely on the rocky outcropping, not budged even by the boisterous sea.

With her forward section caved in and water flowing freely into the bowels of the ship, the captain stopped her engines, ordered a distress call, and prepared her lifeboats. Still, he cautioned his men that none should attempt to board the dories until he gave assent.

Adding continued insult to her predicament, the *Polias* had stranded at low water—so as the evening progressed, the tide drew in with the darkness, frothy seas sending up imposing waves. All these conditions pushed the ship firmer in place, and increasingly "unnatural sounds" rose from deep within her.

Learning of her predicament, the U.S. Coast Guard cutter *Acushnet*, at Rockland Harbor employed in ice-cutting efforts, set off around 11 p.m. for what would prove a plodding, arduous journey amidst ongoing snow squalls and impediments of ice barges.

Meanwhile, Gustave Kairath, a *Polias* crewmember from Brooklyn, had had enough. Disobeying Captain Coughlan, he led a group of eleven to one of the 35-foot metal boats. As they hastily loaded in and dropped into the wild seas, Kairath yelled back to men remaining on deck to join him and save themselves. The infuriated captain responded that they would only die trying to navigate in a small dory in this furor of weather.

But fearing for their lives—and perhaps also the consequences of their mutinous behavior, should they climb back aboard the menaced ship—they pulled away into the impenetrable, stormy night, and were never seen again.

Meanwhile, Captain Lauriat of the *Acushnet* had made progress and approached nearly three-quarters of a mile to the southeast, anchored in twenty fathoms (120 feet). Rescue boats made their way, avoiding the sharp edges of drifting ice shards, and, during a two-hour ordeal, the remaining twenty-seven members of the *Polias* slid down into the dories or managed to lower their own lifeboats into the choppy sea.

And in the weeks, months, and even years that followed, the *Polias* remained lodged in place, continually disintegrating as her remains were jostled and pummeled by the Atlantic. Salvagers were eventually able to dismantle some of her fixtures, but her hull lingered, withering away until it was an unrecognizable, brine-smeared, kelp-clung hulk. Today, she rests in about thirty feet of water off Port Clyde, an active dive site and a unique remnant of military history.

16

THE VEXING PORTLAND LIGHTSHIP

"The reading of a storm is not so bad as the feeling of it."

— Cotton Mather

The ship moved lightly, delicately—parting the dense fog with its bow as if the vapor were a thick curtain, and the vessel itself emerging on an unknown stage.

Finally, the captain made out the welcoming beam of salvation: An indistinct blur of white light that he recognized as a relief buoy sitting at the location of the temporarily-removed Portland Lightship Station. This, he knew, marked the approach to Portland Harbor.

But, as he was to discover mere minutes later, he was gravely mistaken.

One of his lookouts finally realized that the steamship, the *Bay State*, was off course when he heard waves breaking ahead of him (indicating that the boat was perilously close to shore). He alerted the captain, who ordered the ship's engines be reversed.

But it was too late. Seconds later, the steamship collided with a thick, jagged reef and shuddered to a halt.

In those wee hours of the morning of September 23, 1916, what Captain Levi Foren had identified as the Portland Lightship buoy was actually the "Old Anthony" buoy, located four miles farther inland. Due to the poor visibility, he had been sailing much closer to shore than he ever realized or intended.

This disorientation had been further exacerbated by the matter of the removal of the Portland Lightship Station. The lightship had been put into service in 1903—and would remain active until 1971—and was one of a series of measures employed by the U.S. government to help prevent shipwrecks. Equipped with lights and moored in areas considered dangerous to navigation, the lightships acted as de facto floating lighthouses.

The Portland station, however, had been just recently removed for necessary repairs and inspection. In its place in the interim was a red cylindrical buoy that repeatedly flashed and eclipsed in ten second intervals—making it strikingly similar to, and easily confused with, "Old Anthony."

It was not the first time, nor last, that the lightship—or, more fittingly, the lack thereof—confounded even the most seasoned of sailors well-acquainted with Maine's mysterious waters.

Steaming Toward Disaster

The *Bay State* had been born of celebration: She was built in 1894 and launched on September 29 that year to mark the 50th anniversary of the Portland Steam Packet Company (which would later become part of the Eastern Steamship Corporation). The steamship soon began making regular service between Portland and Boston. It was engaged in that duty the fateful night of September 23, 1916, roughly two-hundred-fifty passengers aboard.

At the close of that summer, Foren had replaced the vacationing captain A.B. Strout; a well-liked and respected navigator and leader, Foren had never previously experienced an accident during his time with the steamship company.

Of course, that good fortune was about to end, and in rather dramatic fashion.

That fateful morning, after Foren had incorrectly identified the buoy amidst the dense shroud of fog, the *Bay State* abruptly smacked into a ledge known as Holycomb Reef offshore from Cape Elizabeth.

At the captain's orders, the ship immediately began blasting her steam-powered horn. Its shrill, repeated peals were heard all along the coast, including at Cape Elizabeth Two Lights. Roused from sleep, her passengers, alarmed but surprisingly not panicked, began gathering about the deck, huddling quietly as they awaited orders or news from the bustling crew.

After impact, the ship at first remained upright and seemingly stable—but the combined forces of the tide and wind drove her higher upon the rocks, eventually jabbing her clockwise so that she lay broadside, and perpendicular to shore. Increasingly prone, she began to sway noticeably, her smokestacks and guy wires similarly shaking and quivering.

Then, loud rending noises and thuds emanated from her depths, and her lowermost planking began to give way, allowing water to course freely into the engine room. Foren thus gave orders to douse the steamer's fires and blow the boilers to prevent a deadly explosion.

All the while, locals, interest piqued by the monotonous blare of the wounded steamship's horn, gathered along the beaches to watch the excitement. Fishing boats in the area quickly shuttled in to offer aid; Two Lights keeper Sumner N. Dyer and a rounded-up crew of rescuers also made their way to the ship.

With the ship's rolling and swaying becoming more dramatic every minute, Foren had several of the women and children load into two lifeboats, then lowered them into the water below, where they were shuttled by local fishermen to tugs nearby or the safety of Crescent Beach.

With the arrival of Dyer, meanwhile, the final fourteen members of the crew were hauled to safety via a breeches buoy—a canvas sitting sling attached to a system of lines and pulleys.

Ultimately, all passengers and crew aboard were saved, but the steamship was a loss—and, almost immediately, the shipwreck became a tourist attraction. Spectators from all over rode in on trolleys, taxis, buses, and coaches to get a glimpse of the stranded vessel from the Cape Elizabeth shoreline—where enterprising locals quickly set up popcorn stands and improvised lunch counters. Emblazoned with her moniker, a half-dozen lifeboats and several ropes and pulleys still hanging from her sides, the *Bay State* sat where she had struck, perpendicular to the shoreline, just a few hundred feet out, noticeably listing out toward the bay. Waves continued to pound against her, and over time, her smokestacks sagged together, while paneling, decking, windows and her overall structure canted and slowly caved in on itself.

Eventually, salvagers recovered baggage, cargo and other interior fittings. Later, her twin stacks, boilers, copper, and brass fittings, and anything else of value, was stripped away.

For a time, she remained a shell of a ship left to the elements—rotting and further sinking and lilting at her resting place in the bay, her upper deck eventually giving way to collapse the cabin below. As a precautionary measure, her remains were finally burned.

Shortly after the disaster, a trial ensued. Officials from the Steamboat Inspection Service suspended Foren's pilot's license for three months. The Bureau of Lighthouses, for its part, refused to take any blame for the confusion caused by the removal of the lightship and the placing of near-identical buoys in such close proximity to one another. Nonetheless, though, from that point forward, relief lightships would always replace the Portland Lighthouse whenever she had to be removed (with the exception of a three-year period during World War II).

Still, such human rules had no bearing on Mother Nature and her independent whims.

Deceived by the Tide

The storm that tore in on March 3, 1947, was a wicked one indeed— gusts in the Portland area were clocked at up to eighty miles per hour;

rampant flooding destroyed coastal homes and businesses; ten and fifteen-foot-high snowdrifts blocked roadways, temporarily stranding locals and ceasing commerce; and in some cases power was knocked out for days. The tempest wreaked havoc on local light stations, as well, washing away the bell tower at Saddleback Ledge in Penboscot Bay, besieging the oil house at Matinicus Rock, and tossing aside the fog bell at Portland Head Light—not to mention the widespread damage it caused to keeper's homes and outbuildings.

And the Portland Lightship was not immune: She was dragged and batted about like a toy.

One of the greatest resulting tragedies was that of the *Novadoc*, which simply disappeared amidst the gale. The 261-foot, 2,227-ton Canadian freighter was en route to New York from Digby, Nova Scotia, and carrying a cargo of the mineral gypsum. At 2:48 a.m., her crew sent out a cryptic distress signal: "NOVADOC IN TROUBLE WE ARE TWENTY TWO MILES EAST OF PORTLAND SHIPPING WATER INTO A BROKEN HATCH AND RUNNING BEFORE THE WIND."

Rescue crews received the message, and Coast Guardsmen stationed at Cape Elizabeth also saw distress rockets. They sent out a dispatch to the general area she described, but found nothing. Later, search planes covered 10,000 square miles of ocean. Still nothing—no wreckage, lifeboats, life jackets, any hint of debris—was ever found. All twenty-four crew members aboard, including two female cooks, had been lost.

Also in those predawn hours, the *Oakey L. Alexander* found itself in peril, then in an outright emergency.

With a crew of thirty-two aboard and captained by Raymond Lewis, the cargo ship was owned by the Pocahontas Steamship Co.; she was shuttling 8,200 tons of coal up from Norfolk, Virginia. To this point, she had boasted a long and successful career: This was her 850th round trip between Maine and Virginia.

Snow, rain, and sleet pummeled the boat as it approached Portland. With the storm growing ever fiercer, Lewis and his crew struggled to make out the flash of the Portland Lightship to maintain their bearings and stay on course. Finally, they did spot the lightship—only they didn't know at the time that it had been dragged several miles from its station by ferocious waves.

The *Alexander* thus stayed its course—until smacking directly into an enormous wave that Lewis later described as eighty feet high. The massive wall of water struck the ship around 4:30 a.m. Everyone aboard felt a "sudden lurch," then were throw about violently, as the ship cracked in half. A 135-foot-long portion of the bow had been ripped free. Quickly filling with water, it dangled for a few minutes, moving "up and down like it was elastic," as one eyewitness recalled, then it was ripped free by the waves and immediately sank.

Miraculously, no crew members were aboard this portion of the ship—and in fact, a bulkhead had recently been installed just forward of the split portion, thus sealing the floating half that remained and preventing her from being inundated with water.

Now captaining half a ship, Lewis called for "slow ahead" on the engine, and steered the crippled vessel toward the Cape Elizabeth shore. As they diligently eased the *Alexander* closer and closer to dry land, the crew sent out repeated, five-blast distress signals, and also alerted the Coast Guard. Lewis later commended his crew for their composure, saying that, "No one will ever have a crew as calm as mine. Every man stood by his post."

Around 6:15 a.m., after her crew spotted the fixed and flashing lights of Cape Elizabeth's two light towers, the ship rammed the rocks about 150 yards offshore from the lighthouse. As she came to rest, she listed to her port side, and the heavy waves continued to pound and break against her hull.

As seas were too rough to launch a lifeboat, a crew of Coast Guardsmen—assigned to a lifesaving station adjacent to the lighthouse—readied rescue equipment onshore. Notably, this included a Lyle gun, a small, short-barreled cannon used to fire a line to vessels in distress. Around 8 a.m., the rescuers shot a line out to the ship, which the crew aboard caught and secured to the bridge. A pulley, a hawser (a length of thick cable), and a breeches buoy were then sent across.

Over a tense, two-hour period, the thirty-two members of the *Alexander*'s crew were transported to shore. One-by-one, each climbed into the breeches buoy, which rescuers then used to haul them 600 feet as they dangled above dangerous waves. It took about five minutes to pull each man across; two or three of them, as squalls blew up, were dunked into the freezing, turbulent waters (one for a full harried, hectic twenty seconds).

All told, the *Alexander* suffered no casualties—except, of course, herself. Surviving photos depict her dismal last days: a literally halved ship, fatally wounded, a black, cavernous maw exposing her hollow, empty innards. Waves crashing against her deck, whitecaps foaming all around her, she lazily lilted to her port side, seemingly exhausted by her final exertions.

Again, onlookers showed up by the thousands to get a look at the legendary ship. The news of the rescue was carried in papers all along the coast—one headline from the *Portland Evening Express*, for example, blared: "Oakey L. Alexander Wrecked On Cape Shore; Crew Taken Off" and "Storm Winds Worse Than '38 Hurricane."

Salvagers soon recovered about a thousand tons of coal, while also removing portions of the hull, superstructure, and eventually cutting the ship to water line for scrap. Today, the *Alexander*'s paltry remains lie just off the coast of Two Lights State Park. Her sunken bow section has never been recovered.

And what of the Portland Lightship?

The seething storm had slowly dragged her, anchor and all, all while continually tossing her one way and another. As her captain, Asbury A. Hanna, wrote later: "She stuck her bow down under the heavy seas, and then her stern went under. She pitched and rolled as much as she could. I felt at times as though she wouldn't come back, but she did." He also recalled how a 200-pound safe in his quarters had torn loose from the floor amidst the violent jostling, then "chased me around."

Similarly, frightened crewmen were unable to remain in their bunks as the ship was batted back and forth. They lashed down everything that could move, even the lightest of objects.

Despite their efforts to keep the lightship in place—as dictated by Coast Guard policy, a lightship much stand on station, weather conditions notwithstanding—the vessel broke its anchor, and its crankshaft was also bent. Unable to navigate, the lightship drifting listlessly, its crew dropped a spare anchor, which finally caught, then held firm—luckily, leaving the vessel to dangle less than a mile-and-a-half from a dizzying ledge of granite.

The *Cowslip*, a buoy tender, was able to come to its aid, but it was not for 36 hours, once the weather had slackened, that the lightship could be towed to the harbor for repairs. Amidst that mighty, relentless storm of 1947, the lightship was a rescuer, as it were, for once in need of her own rescue.

17

ENDURING RELICS

"Nothing, I had come to believe by the end, was more
illusory than the idea of ending."

—Clive Barker

They have served as watery tombstones, tangible ghosts: poking
forth from mud and wet sand; sprawling across giant seaside boulders; floating in shallow, rock-strewn waters.

Of the countless vessels tossed, dashed, smashed, or otherwise lost to
time and the elements—sailing off into history, leaving not a frag-
ment of their fate, or plunging deep into the depths of the ocean's chill
clutches—but a few have remained, rotting at their final death ports,
or reemerging with the waxing and waning whims of the sea and her
ceaseless tide.

One notable example of recent memory: the relic of a Revolutionary
War-era sloop at Short Sands Beach in York. Her curved wooden back-
bone and decaying ribs were washed free of their murky entrenchment
following a particularly brutal nor'easter in March 2018. Lodged in
muck and rimmed by rocks, her carcass of warped, toothy ribs—which
once rose up to form her hull—fascinated onlookers, archaeologists, and
historians alike.

The ship's remnants have resurfaced sporadically over the decades, but these infrequent—and brief—protrusions only add to its mystique, according to local historian Sharon Cummins. "Each time, roughly once every decade or two, new maritime history buffs are born," she attested in an editorial.

The artifact initially revealed itself in 1958 before being quickly reburied by the shifting sands and tides. It then reappeared in 1978, at least once or twice more in the latter half of the 20th century, and again during a Patriots' Day storm of 2007. Despite these ever-brief appearances, experts have been able to glean valuable nuggets of information.

Based on the type of construction, she was identified early on by marine archaeologist Warren Riess as a sloop of the Revolutionary age. Further study by Leigh Smith, a historic archaeologist for the Maine Historic Preservation Commission, found that 51 feet of the vessel had been preserved, allowing him to safely presume that she had once been about 60 feet long and 14 feet wide. She was built anywhere between 1750 and 1850, Smith surmised, and had likely been stranded too far ashore to refloat—so she was, it can be assumed, stripped of her goods and abandoned. Her timbers had also clearly been cut by human implements, indicating that the ship was stripped down to the waterline, as was the practice of the time.

As Smith told the *Boston Globe*, her circumstances are hardly unique; vessel remains litter the shorelines of Maine, the majority out of them out of sight and reach. "People just don't know about them either because they're covered with water, or up in Maine, they're covered with seaweed," he said, adding that such cloaking sand, water, flotsam and jetsam actually provide the best means of preservation. Once exposed to the air, artifacts, especially waterlogged wooden ones, are prone to bacteria that can speed up their deterioration.

In the end, not for the lack of effort, little is known of the submerged artifact's origins, destination, crew, cargo—or what ultimately caused her to wreck, strand, or be abandoned. Perhaps the next time she reveals herself—when the weather, sands, and tides are aligned and so inclined—more of her secrets will be coaxed free, as well.

Several miles farther north, the remnants of another wreck have proved much less mysterious—but no less compelling.

Embedded in the sands of Higgins Beach in Scarborough is the corroded skeleton of the *Howard W. Middleton*. The three-masted sailing schooner wrecked off the city's shores amidst near-zero visibility on the night of August 10, 1897, while in the process of shuttling a load of nearly 900 tons of hard and soft coal.

According to witness Emma Bray David, that was a "bad, bad night—foggy! It was so thick it looked as if the space between earth and sky was stuffed with gray-white cotton," she wrote in 1967. After wrecking, the "really noble ship" stayed on the rocks "pretty as a picture" for all the rest of August and the ensuing fall, then broke up sometime over the winter and washed ashore.

A boon for spectators and salvagers alike, some years the ribs of her hull "stand up head high above the beach," Bray David wrote, "and perhaps the next year they will be buried in the sand." Meanwhile, her innards had poured forth beautiful, iridescent shards of coal flecked red, green, and blue, which were collected by locals and vacationers alike. As time proceeded forward, Bray David further reflected, "there are always changes around the old wreck."

Today, the skeletal remains of the once majestic ship appear at times like a stranded primordial beast: Bottom arc firmly entrenched, her timbers bow up out of the sand; warped and jagged, yet thick and strong, they are covered with bright green growths of moss and barnacles, and strewn about with kelp.

Ample—endless—wreckage lies elsewhere, ripe for the finding. At Lobster Cove on Monhegan Island, for instance, there lies a red-rusted portion of the cracked-apart hull of the *D. T. Sheridan*, which stranded and sank in 1948 when carrying coal from Virginia to Bangor. Shifting sands at Gooch's Beach and Mother's Beach in Kennebunk have also at times revealed dim outlines and rusted carcasses of long-lost ships.

Then there are all the hulks and fragments that lie in restless sleep below the tumultuous waters off Maine's shores. Ultimately, the bottom of the ocean is littered with debris—evidence of man's pitiless, attempted domination, nudged about by currents, probed by sea life, becoming less distinguishable as manmade, and ever increasingly wards of the sea. While some of it has been found and explored by divers and underwater archaeologists, so much more remains undiscovered. As Robert Ballard, shipwreck archaeologist and famed discoverer of the legendary RMS *Titanic* once noted, "There's probably more history now preserved underwater than in all the museums of the world combined."

Back up at the surface, though, perhaps the most notorious of the ships left to the sea's abandon—in modern times, at least—were the phantom hulls of the *Luther Little* and *Hesper*.

For more than a half-century, the two vessels sat along the Sheepscot River in Wiscasset, leaning against one another like T.S. Eliot's hollow men. Docked in shallow water, their naked wooden hulls were stripped of lacquer and paint and eaten through by the elements; their bottoms corroding in brine and mud; their masts mere skeletons long divested of their sails.

They were physical attestations to the fact that everything reaches a final use—even, for all the money and effort that goes into them, seafaring vessels. Typically, when no longer deemed seaworthy or no longer needed, ships are dismantled, innards reused, the remainder scrapped; other times they are dry-docked. In some cases, however, as with the *Luther Little* and *Hesper*, they are anchored and left to the whims of nature, taunted by the fact that they remain floating in harbors, coves, rivers or wharves, yet never shall sail again.

With its bustling history of maritime trade, Maine has had a handful of such "ship graveyards"—including what was known as the "Dead Fleet" or "Ghost Fleet," at Mill Cove in Boothbay Harbor; at one point in the 1930s there were nearly a dozen schooners left there to rot, some rafted together to save space.

The "Wiscasset Schooners" *Luther Little* and *Hesper*, for their part, remained in a watery purgatory for 66 years just along the Route 1 bridge in Wiscasset—whose port, in its heyday, rivaled that of Boston—attracting photographers, artists, tourists, scavengers, and those simply intrigued by the abandoned.

Yet few got to see them as they thrived in life.

Both four-masted schooners were built in Somerset, Massachusetts, around the time of the First World War. The 204-foot-long *Luther Little* was launched in December 1917, the 210-foot-long *Hesper* (whose name ancient history aficionados would recognize as a variation of the Greek Hesperus, the evening star) in July 1918.

For much of their early lives, they were used to transport coal, oil, and fertilizer to ports all around the Atlantic.

Then, during the Great Depression, after being inert in Portland Harbor for two years, they were purchased at auction by timber baron Frank Winter. Paying just $1,125 for both of them, he had them repaired and maintained with the intent of using them to transfer lumber cargoes to Boston and New York.

But Winter's operation eventually began to encounter problems too numerous to continue, and the once-majestic ships remained docked. For a time, a watchman lived aboard them; then in 1936 they were dragged closer to shore. There they remained until 1998, slowly ransacked of their usable parts, disintegrating into themselves as the water receded into muck, suffering the ravage of numerous fires.

When their remains were finally cleared away, they had deteriorated from majestic sailing ships into barely-distinguishable rubble. Local craftsmen salvaged what they could and reused scrap for furniture and artwork, while some artifacts ended up at the Maine Maritime Museum and the Somerset Historical Society.

Today they live on in countless images, having been prolifically documented and cataloged as they withered and decayed in plain sight. Some of the most striking images, captured by Lawrence Lufkin, reveal their disintegrating interiors: floors, decks, beams, supporting boards in chaos and confusion; collapsed, pitted, caved-in, rotted-through.

In the end, all that remains of the Wiscasset Schooners is the memory of their wreck and ruin.

SOURCES

I am truly indebted to local historians, authors, and journalists who have dedicated themselves to chronicling Maine's maritime history—notably the ever-prolific Edward Rowe Snow. Thank you for your diligence. I can only hope to do you justice.

Books

Bachelder, Peter Dow, *The Lighthouses and Lightships of Casco Bay*, The Provincial Press, 1995.

-------, *Shipwrecks and Maritime Disasters of the Maine Coast*, The Provincial Press, 1997.

Burbank, Ted, *Maine Shipwrecks, Treasures, Pirates,* Salty Pilgrim Press, 2013 (second edition).

Caldwell, Bill, *Lighthouses of Maine*, Down East Books, 2002.

Clifford, J. Candace and Clifford, Mary Louise, *Women Who Kept the Lights: An Illustrated History of Female Lighthouse Keepers*, Cypress Communications, 1993.

D'Entremont, Jeremy, *Great Shipwrecks of the Maine Coast*, Commonwealth Editions, 2010.

Gratwick, Harry, *Historic Shipwrecks of Penobscot Bay*, The History Press, 2014.

Grenon, Ingrid, *Lost Maine Coastal Schooners: From Glory Days to Ghost Ships*, The History Press, 2010.

Hughes, Patricia, *Lost Loot: Ghostly New England Treasure Tales*, Schiffer Publishing Ltd., 2008.

Miller, Nathan, *Sea of Glory: The Continental Navy Fights for Independence, 1775-1783*, D. McKay Co., 1974.

Quinn, William P., *Shipwrecks Around Maine*, The Lower Cape Publishing Co., 1983.

-------, William P., *Shipwrecks Around New England*, The Lower Cape Publishing Co., 1979.

Snow, Edward Rowe, *Great Storms and Shipwrecks of the New England Coast*, The Yankee Publishing Company, originally published 1943.

-------, Edward Rowe, *Legends of the New England Coast*, Dodd, Mead & Company, 1957.

-------, *The Lighthouses of New England*, Dodd, Mead and Company, 1945, 1973.

-------, Edward Rowe, *Marine Mysteries and Dramatic Disasters of New England*, Dodd, Mead & Company, 1976.

Sterling, Robert Thayer, *Lighthouses of the Maine Coast and the Men Who Kept Them*, The Stephen Daye Press, 1935.

Warner, Mark, *The Tragedy of the Royal Tar: Maine's 1836 Circus Steamboat Disaster*, Warner Publishing, 2010.

Welner, Stacy L., *Tragedy in Casco Bay*, Anchor Publishing, 2006.

Newspaper/Web-based Articles

Cartwright, Steve, "'Grand Design' lured 18th century immigrants to a tragic end," *The Working Waterfront Archives*, March 1, 2006.

Cummins, Sharon, "Skeleton of sunken ship laid bare at York's Short Sands Beach," Seacoastonline.com, March 13, 2013.

Curtis, Abigail, "Maine's own Thanksgiving story: How the Indians saved 18th century shipwreck victims," *The Bangor Daily News*, November 28, 2013.

Dwyer, Dialynn, "Here's what is known about the shipwreck unearthed by a nor'easter in Maine," *The Boston Globe*, March 9, 2018.

Hanna, David, "The sea fight that inspired a Longfellow poem," *The Atlantic*, January 3, 2012.

Sharp, David, "Navy vessel sunk by German sub in WWII finally found," *The Associated Press*, July 18, 2019.

"The Shipwrecks of Maine," Maine Public Radio Network, original air date, September 19, 2019, mainepublic.org.

"Shipwreck found in Black Sea is 'world's oldest intact,'" *BBC News*, October 23, 2018.

"The story of the wreck, as told by Emma Bray David," December 1967, Higginsbeachmaine.com.

Websites

American Lighthouse Foundation, lighthousefoundation.org
Atlas Obscura, atlasobscura.com
Maine Memory Network, mainememory.net
Mount Desert Island Historical Society, mdihistory.org
New England Lighthouses: A Virtual Guide, newenglandlighthouses
    .net
New England Historical Society, newenglandhistoricalsociety.com
Penobscot Bay History Online, penobscotmarinemuseum.org

ABOUT THE AUTHOR

Taryn Plumb is a journalist and author based outside of Portland, Maine, who has always been fascinated with history. Intrigued by the paranormal, she is also the author of *Haunted Boston*, *Haunted Maine Lighthouses*, and *New England UFOs*.